# Reaching a New Generation

## Strategies for Tomorrow's Church

## ALAN J. ROXBURGH

INTERVARSITY PRESS
DOWNERS GROVE, ILLINOIS 60515

InterVarsity Press® is the book-publishing division of InterVarsity Christian Fellowship®, a student movement active on campus at hundreds of universities, colleges and schools of nursing in the United States of America, and a member movement of the International Fellowship of Evangelical Students. For information about local and regional activities, write Public Relations Dept., InterVarsity Christian Fellowship, 6400 Schroeder Rd., P.O. Box 7895, Madison, WI 53707-7895.

Cover illustration: Roberta Polfus

ISBN 0-8308-1340-3

Printed in the United States of America ∞

Library of Congress Cataloging-in-Publication Data

Roxburgh, Alan J.
   Reaching a new generation: strategies for tomorrow's church/
  Alan J. Roxburgh.
     p.   cm.
  Includes bibliographical references.
  ISBN 0-8308-1340-3
   1. Postmodernism—Religious aspects—Christianity.
  2. Christianity and culture.   3. Human ecology—Religious aspects—
  Christianity.  4. Spirituality.  5. Christianity—20th century.
  I. Title.
  BT28.R685     1993
  261—dc20                     92-34569
                                CIP

| 17 | 16 | 15 | 14 | 13 | 12 | 11 | 10 | 9 | 8 | 7 | 6 | 5 | 4 | 3 | 2 | 1 |
|----|----|----|----|----|----|----|----|----|----|----|----|----|----|----|----|----|
| 06 | 05 | 04 | 03 | 02 | 01 | 00 | 99 | 98 | 97 | 96 | 95 | 94 | 93 | | | |

86746

# INTRODUCTION ———————————————

# The
# Big
# Carrot

T his book began with a simple goal. After I had served as pastor of a growing downtown church for several years, a health-food store opened its doors a block away. Within a short time the Big Carrot became the busiest place in the neighborhood. This instant popularity represented more than just people's interest in health foods. I wanted to understand it, so I undertook a study.

I assumed my undertaking would be a simple investigation leading to evangelistic strategies. But I was wrong; the issues were much larger. I soon uncovered difficult questions for the church's witness in our culture. Gradually I came to recognize that my primary need was not to develop evangelistic strategies to reach the people who frequented the Big Carrot but to understand the underlying questions raised by the popularity and growth of this small health food store. The Big Carrot was like a barometer, reflecting important value and meaning changes for many in our society.

This book is written from the perspective of a pastor turned teacher who is struggling to articulate a theology for congregational mission in a changing situation. Often Christians insist that we need to recover the biblical pattern of the church. They assume that we have lost God's intention for the church and this is the root of our malaise. But this is only part of the story. North American churches have lost touch with the incredible changes that have been transforming our culture over the past twenty-five years. Consequently, we are ill-prepared to speak the gospel into the world taking shape about us.

We are in a new time of mission in North America. The outlines of what lies ahead are not yet clear. It is important to discern the shape of the road ahead and suggest ways a congregation may engage this changing context with the message of Jesus Christ.

There is an increasing recognition that the modern world is in a period of fundamental change in terms of values, spiritual consciousness and worldview. This book will examine the implications of these changes as they are expressed in the context of a health food mall. But the sweeping cultural changes are being recognized at many levels. When Peter Drucker looks at the political, economic and knowledge changes in our society, he concludes that "there are new realities." He goes on: "Some time between 1965 and 1973 we passed over such a divide and entered 'the next century.' " We have passed by the creeds and commitments that had shaped us for over a century, he says, and traveled into a land that is "terra incognita" with few familiar landmarks to guide us.[1] While Drucker is speaking specifically of the political context, he could have used the same language for science, spirituality and our relationship with the created world. We have moved into a terra incognita.

Cultural critic O. B. Hardison Jr. writes about change in modern culture as having been fundamental; the familiar vocabularies, concepts and images we had come to take for granted are no longer viable. As the title of his recent book *Disappearing Through a Skylight* suggests, what we had come to consider as the real world has, as it were, vanished. He asks:

Is the idea of what is human disappearing, along with so many other ideas, through the modern skylight? . . . In its fearless exploration of inner and outer worlds, modern culture has evidently reached a turning point—a kind of phase transition from one set of values to another.[2]

A turning point from one set of values to another—almost the same language Drucker used to describe the changes he sees from a very different perspective.

Social forces at work today are bringing a new kind of consciousness to life, and many are wondering whether a whole new array of values and beliefs can transform the modern world. Those who have become disenchanted with the process of secularization but see no hope in traditional Christianity are seeking alternative models of hope to redefine society in ways which, they believe, will address the confusing and difficult challenges of our day. There is a call for fundamental changes in our value systems and new ways of relating to the natural world.

Geneticist David Suzuki and journalist Anita Gordon argue that the ecological crisis is "forcing us to reexamine the value system that has governed our lives for at least the past 200 years."[3] They describe "sacred truths"—fundamental assumptions—that have shaped our society for generations; these include the belief that nature is infinite, human beings are to have dominion over nature, growth is progress, and we are called to multiply our race. These beliefs, they say, are destroying the planet. "We don't see that our current beliefs and values are right now compromising the very systems that keep us alive. Like Samson blinded, we are straining at the pillars of life and bringing them down around us."[4] And so these values are to be abandoned in the name of survival.

Gordon and Suzuki join a chorus of voices documenting and calling for a turning from one set of values to another, from one view of reality to a new one. Robert Ornstein and Paul Ehrlich argue that the world being presently created is so new and so different from the old values and worldviews that we need a whole new way of thinking if we are to successfully negotiate the current global crisis. In fact, they say, we must "replace our old minds with new ones."[5] The message is clear: the old worldviews cannot sustain us, and we now require new ways of thinking and valuing.

Christian thinkers are also mapping this unsettling journey into change. Diogenes Allen speaks of the breakdown of the modern mentality. He claims that we are in the midst of a massive intellectual revolution, similar to the one that marked off the Middle Ages from the modern period.[6] James B. Miller agrees, saying that Western civilization is going through a shift in its worldview even though the emerging worldview still remains unclear.[7] Christian thinkers as diverse as Lesslie Newbigin, Richard Neuhaus, Stanley Hauerwas, Langdon Gilkey and Hans Küng all speak of an important cultural turning point—a transformation that requires us to find new ways of reaching a new generation.

Beginning in a local context, this book examines how change and transformation challenge the church to rethink its mission in the modern world. I will argue that important elements of modernity are being rejected by the culture, and that a search for alternative values is gaining momentum. A number of factors contribute to this process.

First, there is a growing disillusionment with the technological society produced by scientific rationalism. Some readers may wish to dispute this idea. Robert Wuthnow has in fact argued that since World War II technology has become the legitimating myth that has replaced civil religion.[8] The myth of inevitable development accompanies the modern faith in technology, along with the belief in manifest destiny. For Wuthnow, technology has become the basic structural and ideological feature of modern life. Like the medieval church, it has become an omnipresent influence that reaches into all of life; yet because it is so pervasive, it is taken for granted. In this sense technology becomes the sacred canopy, the overarching legitimating myth of the culture.

Wuthnow is correct in his analysis of the state of North American culture since World War II. But there is increasing evidence that technology as a legitimating myth is itself beginning to come under severe critical evaluation. Green movements, the celebration of Earth Day and the growing quest for ways of living in harmony with nature evidence a disenchantment with technology as our culture's legitimating myth.

This does not mean that the culture is denying technology's necessary role in the development of society. What we are discussing is a disenchantment with technology as an end in itself. We are facing the recognition that technology has failed to provide us with the kind of life we expected. Progress has not brought greater freedom or control over life but increasing rates of crime, greater social stratification, gridlocked cities, malfunctioning urban infrastructures and a poisoned atmosphere. In spite of real advances in medicine and convenience, people now sense that technology and progress have given us a society of useless products, deforested countryside, polluted water, extinct species and fragmented social structures.

This may be a one-sided perspective, failing to account for the tremendous good technology has brought. But an emerging consensus suggests that, on balance, scientific rationalism and its applications in technology have brought us ecodestruction and human fragmentation. Technology is being seriously questioned as the legitimating myth of our culture.

Second, despite the apparent reemergence of evangelicalism in North America, increasing numbers of people are turning away from traditional Christianity.[9] The search for spiritual values has not led to a renewal of traditions; instead, people are integrating alternative religious experiences into their belief systems. In an urbanized, pluralistic society of relativized choice, many people show little interest in Christianity, for they perceive it as powerless in the present crisis. The new spiritualities are generally an amalgam of popular psychology, mysticism, the new science and traditional Christianity.

It's clear that Constantinianism has lost its residual power. We are witnessing a breakdown of consensus within what has been identified as the civil religion of North America. Attempts to recapture Christendom will not effectively engage this process of worldview change. We will need other ways of engaging a new generation.

Third, certain cultural and global shifts fuel the current experience of fragmentation and insecurity. Movements emphasizing rights, choice and equality challenge the older, static order of the Christian consensus; the ecological movement questions the assumptions of dominance and control rooted in Western theology and language; the redefining of the scientific paradigm is radically altering perceptions of truth. Shifts in world order and power—from North America and the Atlantic perimeter to South Asia and the Pacific Rim—are creating a deepened insecurity and fragmentation, while Western Christianity is further marginalized. The search for fresh visions of human society, for values and beliefs to shape our survival, continues. We are witnessing the emergence of a culture in search of paradigms to shape its life. In this process of experimentation, belief systems of the recent past are being cast aside, judged impotent to carry us into the future.

Fourth, secularism is being reshaped. As a pluralistic value system, secularism assumes all truths are relative, contingent upon the time, place and history of individuals and cultures.

Up until the nineteenth century, it was religion that shaped the fundamental worldview of culture in the West. Since then a whole series of other forces have gradually replaced this worldview with the symbols of scientific rationalism and material progress. [It was not that religion ceased to be present in the culture; it was that religion ceased to have a *shaping effect* on the culture. It was not that people ceased to believe in God, but that this belief ceased to have much practical effect on life.] So there emerged another worldview, which we have come to identify as the secular. Secularism involves a sharp separation between the material and the religious, between value and fact, faith and reason.

But the secular assumptions no longer hold, and secularism is itself being transformed into something else. Secularism erodes traditional religious foundations but cannot abolish the thirst for spiritual direction.

While traditional religious institutions lose credibility in the Western world, people search for alternatives or reshape Christian beliefs into a more syncretistic commitment. This provides fertile ground for spiritualities that significantly challenge the church.

These factors are present in the context of the Big Carrot health food store, the setting for this work. We will discover that the Big Carrot is a symbol of disillusionment with technology and its applications to nutrition. It also symbolizes the search for alternative spirituality. The formation of the Big Carrot as a business cooperative suggests the desire to overcome fragmentation and discover models of life and work that are connective and holistic. Finally, its openness to many values around a common desire to make the world a better place illustrates how secularism is moving into new forms of syncretistic spirituality.

But the Big Carrot is only one illustration of the coming together in a search for new paradigms. In England, the area around Glastonbury has become a center for alternative values and spiritualities. It is fascinating to recognize that, according to legend, St. Paul sent Joseph of Arimathea to England, where he founded the first church at Glastonbury. Today that same locale is the seedbed for a rejection of Christianity and a search for transformative values.

Charing Cross, London, is a street filled with expansive bookstores. In these shops the sections on religion and spirituality have grown very large over the past several years. But what is most arresting about these sections is the character of the material. By far the largest collection of books deals with issues of spiritual transformation and unitive wholeness from non-Christian perspectives. Sometimes such books are based on Eastern mysticism, but more often today people seem to be seeking an integration of science and spirituality. A visit to bookstores in any large urban center in North America will show the same kind of presence.

It's not that the 1980s gave rise to new religious groups that can be easily identified. Rather, a *new set of values* has begun to shape the discussion about the paradigm needed to inform our culture as it moves through transition. The conversation is everywhere, but is often not named as such.

Wherever you go across North America, you will find a proliferation of health food stores and bookstores that are generative centers and gathering points for the conversation. If you listen with attentiveness, you'll discover that people are reading and talking about the kinds of beliefs and values that will move us away from destructive fragmentation and ecological disaster. And the overarching legitimating story of Christianity is not the framework shaping these conversations.

It is important to define two terms used throughout this book: *culture* and *modernity*. The term *culture* is an ambiguous one. H. Richard Niebuhr established a series of categories to describe the ways in which the church relates to its surrounding culture. While I tend toward a perspective of the Christ who transforms culture, my use of the term *culture* in this book does not follow Niebuhr's analysis. The term has an interesting history of development with the emergence of the social sciences in the nineteenth century. Peter Schineller defines it in this way: "a set of symbols, stories (myths) and norms for conduct that orient society to the world in which it lives."[10] Culture is the worldview of a people, all the learned behavior that makes sense of our world and makes us at home in the group to which we belong. It is that ongoing process whereby we produce meanings out of our social experience—meanings that give us place and identity in the wider world. Culture is implicit, like the superstructure of a building; it is essential but hidden from view. It is what we use to look at the world, the glasses through which we see and order our world.

It can be argued that there are many cultures shaping life in North America. But there is also a pervasive underlying culture, and this we are calling *modernity*. This term is generally used to describe the social and intellectual culture that has shaped Western life for nearly three hundred years. Its basic characteristics are familiar to us all, so familiar that we take them for granted and assume that things have always been this way. Modernity is characterized by its commitments to technical rationality and individualism. We highly value the right of individuals to choose for themselves their direction in life, untrammeled by hierarchy and authority. This is a canon of our culture: the individual rights of every human being are sacred so long as they do not trample on the rights of others. Our liberal democracies are built upon this fundamental presupposition of modernity. Further, modernity has been characterized by the pervasive power of science and a strong faith in technology's ability to achieve an ever-developing progress. In the midst of these two concerns, modernity is also shaped by its commitment to the secular. This does not imply disbelief in the supernatural, but an assumption that the important elements of life are in the material here and now.

Thomas Oden provides this evaluation of modernity:

Modernity is a period, a mindset, and a malaise. The period begins with the French Revolution in 1789. The mindset is that ethos reflected by an elitist intellectual class of "change agents." . . . [Its] four fundamental values are moral relativism (which says that what is right is dictated by culture, social location and situation), autonomous individualism (which assumes that moral authority comes essentially from within), narcissistic hedonism (which focuses on egocentric personal pleasure), and reductive naturalism (which reduces what is reliably known to what one can see, hear and empirically investigate). The malaise of modernity is related to the rapidly deteriorating influence of these values.[11]

As cultural critics have often pointed out, the church itself has largely become captive to the assumptions of modernity and has lost its own sense of identity. As society searches for new norms, the church needs to recognize this captivity and allow God's Word to shape it in a new context.

The emergence and rapid growth of a relatively small business like the Big Carrot symbolize the drive to reexamine formative values. It is representative of what can be found throughout Europe and North America: small organizations and movements searching for a new consciousness, a worldview with which to transform Western culture.

# ONE

# Change,
# Growth,
# Challenge

T he early 1980s were a time of change in North America. Cities and people were in flux. The energy crisis of the 1970s, along with the economic recovery that began the 1980s, changed attitudes about urban living. Many people moved back into the downtown neighborhoods their parents had left in the postwar shift to the suburbs. The new city dwellers were looking for more than fuel savings through shorter commutes. They wanted to develop new lifestyles in a society that seemed to be going terribly wrong. The suburbs had ceased to be the beckoning future; something had gone amiss with the postwar dream of an ever-better life in vast new housing developments. In downtown areas, the noise of hammers and drills as old houses were rehabbed suggested that young adults were looking for different values with which to shape their lives.

Many churches in these downtown neighborhoods were far from healthy. They had become dwindling gatherings of aging members clinging to a disappeared past. In the fall of 1981 I began pastoral leadership in one such church, Danforth Baptist. From its heyday in the early fifties, when some four hundred people had packed its sanctuary each Sunday, it had dwindled to a congregation of about thirty. Mostly senior citizens, the members of Danforth Baptist had no idea what had happened to their church or why the neighborhood where they had grown up and married now seemed crowded with strangers speaking other languages.

With all the innocence and arrogance of youth, I accepted the challenge of leading this church. The initial years were demanding and painful. We saw friends become strangers, visions crumble and ego collide with ego. Yet God was amazingly gracious. The church began to grow and be renewed. Eventually Danforth grew to about 240 people in several congregations, committed to a vision of mission through church planting. A large percentage of Danforth's members came to live in the immediate neighborhood. Half the members were now under thirty-five, and 70 percent were under forty-five. We became a young congregation in age and history, having discovered that God can bring life to an old downtown church.

Growth came through such things as dynamic worship, contemporary music and praise, nurture and mission groups, outreach ministries, team leadership and an openness to all that the Spirit wanted to give and say to us through one another. One outreach ministry, called the Danforth Café, was designed to present contemporary themes and issues in an informal, nonthreatening atmosphere where people could discuss faith and values. Through the café we touched non-Christians from both the neighborhood and the larger city. Operating biweekly, this ministry addressed issues such as refugee needs, sexual abuse, housing, the environment, spirituality and values. Excellent music and other arts were a major component in its life. Each evening the café was open some seventy people, most from outside the church, crowded into a refurbished room to engage in conversation, listen to lectures on important issues or just enjoy good music.

In cooperation with a government agency, we initiated a housing project for economically disadvantaged single adults. Four large rehabbed houses were opened to about eight residents each. A number of the residents eventually joined our cell groups and became active in the church as a result of the friendships and care they received from Christians. Danforth also developed a counseling ministry that not only responded to needs in the congregation but also served the neighborhood.

And so from the stump of an aging, dying congregation God chose to grow a new shoot full of beautiful new life. For those of us involved in this transformation it was a hard but wonderful birth. We were changed in ways that none of us could have ever imagined. We came to recognize that renewal is not a function of the brightest and best bringing their marvelous ideas for change and growth. God uses those who, through brokenness and pain, discover his love and direction. He takes our great weakness and turns it into life through Christ.

## Competing Visions

But as Danforth Baptist flourished in its renewal, new and troubling challenges were emerging in the neighborhood—challenges the church was ill-prepared to face. Two years after I began my pastorate at Danforth, another new group arrived and began to build a different sort of community just one block down from the church. Soon it seemed that two forms of renewal were taking place, one in the church and the other in the Big Carrot, the new health food store down the street. While a group of Christians sought to recover vitality in worship and mission, the folks involved with the Big Carrot pursued their dream of making the world a better place. Each of these two communities was pursuing a dream bigger than itself, and, maybe without recognizing the fact, each was asking the larger community of city dwellers which of these dreams best fit their longings and needs.

Until recently, churches had been the primary value-generating centers of North American society. But this is no longer true. As John Naisbitt and

Patricia Aburdene have correctly indicated, the church has moved from the mainline to the fringes of society, and in its place has emerged a diffuse search for fresh values and directions to address the growing crises of the Western world.[1] It seemed that the dream being forged in the Big Carrot, just down the street from a renewing church, was increasingly attractive to the newly arrived "gentrifying" population.

The Big Carrot proved to be very different from all the other stores on the street. Outwardly, it looked like any other health food store. But it was more than just a place to buy organic foods or morning-glory muffins loaded with "seeds and weeds." The Big Carrot was a concretized vision of the way ordinary people, concerned about the environment and wanting to change certain destructive patterns of modern living, could act creatively to make the world a better place. Very quickly it attracted a growing clientele. The fresh, bright, attractive store, created by the dreams and hard work of the owners rather than some marketing design firm, soon had lineups of faithful customers. The store had touched something in the community that went far beyond the desire for trendy health foods.

At one level, the Big Carrot could be viewed as a successful business story. But there was a lot more to it than the desire to make money. The people who developed the store were not business executives who had researched yuppie tastes with the prime aim of making a lot of money. Those planning the Big Carrot were shaped by significant priorities and values. They wanted a workers' cooperative in which the management and operational staff were also owners. This was to be a hands-on, high-involvement venture. The people one met stocking shelves, preparing food and working at the cash register were also the dreamers and owners who had invested their savings to bring this dream to birth. The co-op was to be a model for an alternative way of working and doing business in the city. Decisions were to be made by consensus; profits would be shared based on labor as well as ownership.

An illustration of this commitment to values greater than profit was the "Venture Capital Fund"[2] the Big Carrot established. The fund uses part of the store's profit to help other business cooperatives get a start. The dream is that out of the fund will come ways for people to deal with pressing social problems. There is a policy of rotating management to maintain equality of function and ownership within the group. In principle, any member could become a manager for a set term, then return to another function in the store.

The cooperative's owners clearly articulated their assumptions about the store's central values. In a segmented, specialized society they recognized the need for integration and wholeness. As one reporter said, where "business, government, labour and education are separated from each other, frustration and misunderstanding result." The Big Carrot brings different interest groups together and "promotes a crossing of boundaries."[3]

By 1987 the Big Carrot had become so successful that it purchased an empty car-sales lot across the street from the church and constructed a mall called the Carrot Common. A variety of stores and services in the mall began operating under an ethos that can be summed up in one key word: wholeness. Included in this ethos are care about what is eaten and how it is produced, concern for the environment, a quest for holistic health, the ideal of crossing boundaries to form coalitions, the attempt to design a work environment in which all workers have a say about the business. All of these concerns can be seen as a response to the alienation and fragmentation of urban life. The Carrot Common offers a variety of goods and services but also, equally important, a value system and a way of life.

As a pastor, I was forced to ask why this store had become so popular so quickly. Clearly it was touching levels of felt need among people of the area and offering a model for change with which people identified. I developed a study project to research people's interest in the store. My intention was to devise strategies for evangelism. But as I continued to visit the Carrot Common, interview shoppers and talk with its board members, I realized that I needed to listen to these people, to hear their views, dreams and questions, before embarking on any evangelization strategy.

The Carrot Common became an opportunity to understand a neighborhood's changing values. The people using the store reflected the community. The largest group were women between the ages of twenty and forty (60 percent), evenly distributed across the income ranges from under $20,000 to more than $60,000 per year. Since food costs at the Carrot were significantly higher than elsewhere in the area, people shopping there were making choices based on values other than cost. Eighty percent of the customers lived less than five kilometers away, mostly in the city's downtown. Generally, they were university-trained and now working in the professions, arts and business. Many were self-employed. Seventy percent of the shoppers surveyed had been coming to the Carrot for longer than a year; a majority of the group had been using the store for three to four years. I also spoke with many enthusiastic first-time shoppers who had heard about the store through referrals. Sixty percent visited the store on a regular weekly basis; it was an important focal point in their lives.

What I discovered through my research was both challenging and troubling. On the basis of interviews and discussion, it was possible to identify three areas of concern that led to people's choice to shop at the Big Carrot: the environment, the search for community and the quest for empowerment.

## Green Values

A recurrent theme expressed by Carrot customers was a concern for the environment. When asked why they chose to shop at the Carrot, they frequently responded with words like *natural, chemical-free, nutritious* and *healthy*. Many expressed concern about carcinogens in foods that were not organically grown. Words like *quality* and *choice* were used in reference to organically grown, chemical-free foods. Shopping at the Carrot was a proactive response to the environment.

Carrot shoppers believed that the store was helping them gain control over the food they ate. But the issues went beyond personal survival. People shopped at the Carrot because it embodied an alternative value system regarding food production and processing. It allowed them to reject an agricultural system they believed to be environmentally abusive and personally dangerous, while affirming their hope and conviction that environmental change could come through local action.

### Building Connections

I had expected Carrot shoppers to be concerned about the environment. But the high value they placed on community formation was surprising. When asked why they shopped at the Carrot, many cited the fact that it was organized as a workers' cooperative. Others were pleased to spend their money at an intentionally small, local business. One person enthusiastically described the Carrot as a community center.

The use of the term *community* symbolizes a search for an integrated, connected life at the local level. Endorsement of the Carrot as a model of community formation implies a critique of large, impersonal corporate structures that focus on profit while affording little sense of community.

### Empowerment

A third reason people gave for their loyalty to the Big Carrot was *empowerment*. While the word was not used directly, the concern was expressed in a variety of ways. Some described the Big Carrot as a place where a small group of ordinary people could create a meaningful business. Others saw the worker-owned cooperative as a sign of control, as opposed to the impersonal forces in large corporations. Even the ability to choose organically grown foods was described as an act of empowerment.

The other stores in the mall further illustrated this theme. One shop not only offered brightly colored crystals but also claimed that possessing and using them could release spiritual power. A yoga institute offered spiritual and meditative techniques to harmonize one's body with the cosmos. A shiatsu clinic promised the same result through somewhat different means,[4] and a health institute offered people methods to enhance their own powers and connect with the fundamental rhythms of nature.

As I listened to the reasons why people found the Carrot Common attractive, it became clear that these highly successful neighborhood busi-nesses, with their varied attempts to articulate a new consciousness, were illustrating and struggling with the sociocultural changes that numerous commentators had begun to identify as characteristic of our time. Pro-prietors of the Carrot Common seemed to have understood the malaise of modernity, and their businesses represented hope of a new way.

Some of the answers they offered may be troubling to Christian disciples. But I realized that if the church was to respond to the concerns represented by the Carrot Common, we would need to understand where these con-cerns had come from and why they touched a chord in so many people. In chapter two I will try to lay the foundations for such an understanding.

# TWO ————————————

# Making the World a Better Place

An ink drawing is often used to show how perspective determines what we see. The drawing is the head of a woman. But the person could be either a beautiful young woman or an old crone, depending on how you look at it. Some will see one image, others another. Many can see both only if the figures are outlined for them.

This issue of perspective, of seeing what is happening before us, is important to our discussion of value transformation. Take the Carrot Common. From one perspective, the mall can be seen as simply a health food store surrounded by an assemblage of other stores that reflect commitment to alternative values. But careful examination of the mall suggests that this characterization is inadequate. If we look closely at the primary images of the health food store, another picture begins to form, and our perspective shifts.

So let's consider what the Big Carrot is all about. It sells food. There are rows upon rows of vegetables and other foodstuffs. Signs describe where and how the food was grown. Pure, naturally grown peanut butter stands beside containers of honey of all kinds. Down one aisle run rows and rows of neatly ordered bins. They contain a wide variety of flours, seeds, herbs and spices. The first-time shopper is amazed to find such an array of choice in natural foodstuffs.

Freshly baked breads and all kinds of macrobiotic foodstuffs are laid out appealingly in another area of the store. A long counter displays organically grown meats and free-range chicken. One section of the store is set aside for an array of books on everything from vegetarian cooking to "natural" remedies for physical ailments. There is even a cosmetic and beauty counter offering a range of natural products. The overall atmosphere is bright, pleasant and inviting.

Food is an important symbol in understanding the Big Carrot. In seeing how food shapes and interprets the Carrot's life, we discern the meaning of this symbol. A Carrot board member mused that if there was a single focus driving the store's operation, it was to supply people with the very best food products that could be obtained. Those who run the Big Carrot are convinced that foods available at traditional supermarkets are full of preservatives and were grown in environments saturated with chemical fertilizers for fast growth, pesticides to kill insects or drugs to enhance livestock growth. If these foods have not been irradiated, then they have endured prolonged storage, further reducing their natural goodness. But the Big Carrot, he said, wants to get back to reasonable standards of food productivity and quality. So all foods sold in the Carrot are organically grown and free from additives. The store is committed to providing food that is free of artificial growth stimulants and pesticides.

Behind this operational philosophy lies the conviction that current food-production techniques poison people and destroy the environment. Big Carrot owners and customers believe that the values that produced Love Canal and polluted the Niagara escarpment with chemical toxins are the same values behind the foods on supermarket shelves. People need to change this pervasive value system by challenging the assumptions and technologies guiding food production and land use.

Food at the Big Carrot is a symbol of the belief that ordinary people can change an essentially destructive society. The Carrot Common, at every level of its organization and practice, proclaims that the world is in deep trouble, and it offers a positive, individually accessible alternative way of living.

All this makes the Carrot stores deeply attractive. They function as both a critique of values endemic in contemporary society and an alternative for those who want new values.

The working environment of the Big Carrot reflects a similar commitment to value changes. The board member with whom I spoke articulated another goal of the Carrot as providing the best possible working environment for people, based on cooperation and self-determination. Again, this principle springs from an analysis of the culture and a desire to do something about its deficiencies. People at the Carrot Common believe that typical modern working environments are sterile, failing to offer people wholeness and integration. The Carrot's alternative ethos says work is something "we do together." And sharing investment and tasks helps make that happen.

Entering the Carrot is a different experience from entering most supermarkets. There is a warm, inviting atmosphere. Employees don't point to where a product can be found; they take you there, show you the products and enter into conversation. They are well informed about their products. This seems to be more than a business strategy; it arises from beliefs about the nature of work and relationships. In this sense the Big Carrot is a laboratory in working community rather like the monasteries of the Middle Ages. The monasteries operated businesses, but their influence resulted from their sense of common belonging within a value-creating community that had intentionally chosen to be an alternative presence in the culture. The Big Carrot is far from being a medieval monastic order, but it shares some of the rationale and attractiveness that must have made those institutions centers of change and transformation.

One board member described the Big Carrot as a group of people who "just wanted to make the world a better place in which to live." That, he said, is "quite central to who we are."

At the Carrot Common there isn't only one way to go about this task, and no one philosophy provides all the answers. But there is one unifying theme: seeking to make the world a better place. Behind this commitment is the belief that much in our present culture works to hinder the healing of people and the planet. There is a belief at the Carrot Common that we need to embrace new ways of living together.

Despite their dissatisfaction with the status quo, these people do not seem to be "cursing the darkness." On the contrary, they see themselves as lighting candles of hope. They are taking explicit, well-thought-out steps to forge new directions in the culture. The anger and militancy that characterized the student movements of the sixties are missing, even though many of the Carrot Common's owners and patrons were involved in those movements. They have developed into a thoughtful and determined group of people. They have a sense that social change comes quietly.

The Carrot Common exudes an atmosphere of optimism and hope. It's a place where idealism is alive and well. This is not some despondent group huddled in a corner, protecting their personal space against the ever-encroaching tide of darkness. There is no hint of self-protectionism or a survivalist mentality. On the contrary, the mall is a place of hope and confidence.

The name Carrot Common is a play on words. *Carrot* refers to the health food store at the center of the project, while *Common* suggests a style of housing or a piece of land open to shared, public use. Thus, the mall is an open area shared by a variety of groups. In addition, the name is a statement of the central Big Carrot ethos. A variety of groups with a variety of philosophies have clustered in one place because they hold a common commitment: to make the world a better place in which to live.

I've already mentioned a few of the other stores that are a part of the Carrot Common, but a closer look will help us see the larger context of this affiliation of businesses. A holistic health center offers advice and direction on wholeness and health that draws on various medical philosophies; a shiatsu center whose massage therapy integrates Eastern understandings of how the body works and heals itself; Kripola Yoga, an institute that teaches a meditative technique for self-development and spiritual enlightenment.

A Carrot Common store called Gifts from the Earth sells nothing but crystals and does an active business. At first glance it appears to be simply an interesting gathering place with a lot of pretty colored stones and bits of glass for sale. But many people have come to ascribe spiritual powers to gemstones. They believe that quartz vibrations, for example, amplify the body's natural electrical current. Crystals, it is claimed, promote healing and are helpful for dealing with stress. Rock singer Tina Turner clutched quartz crystals to help her deal with anxiety during a nationwide concert tour. Crystals are claimed to channel power that can focus meditation and deepen a sense of oneness with the whole of creation. It is claimed that they will remove blocked thought patterns and old childhood hurts, as well as put you in touch with the reasons behind negative behavior patterns.

But the crystal shop should not be casually dismissed as a gimmick. It reflects people's quest for some means of being connected to larger nonmaterial realities. Along with the other stores at Carrot Common, it manifests an underlying search for values that will reconnect people with the earth, one another and hidden spiritual forces. This quest rejects the view of the world as dead, inert material for human consumption and use.

Other Carrot Common businesses include an excellent bookstore, a children's clothing store, a Japanese restaurant and a wonderful coffee shop. Upstairs is the Bread and Roses Credit Union, an alternative banking service that provides loans for new businesses based upon the values of the Carrot Common.

All of this is indicative of a change in outlook which some are calling a paradigm shift in understanding. The Carrot Common symbolizes a shift in worldview.

Our *worldview* defines how we read and understand the world. It is the way a culture conceptualizes reality. James Sire defines worldview as "a set of presuppositions . . . we hold (consciously or subconsciously) about the basic makeup of our world."[1] The process of reassessing and changing worldview presuppositions is taking place at the Carrot Common and all across North America.

So as I investigated the Common, I had a growing sense that I'd stumbled into far larger issues than I had anticipated. The question of how to evangelize in this context was no longer simple to answer. The mall compelled me to ask larger questions about the issues and forces shaping shifts in worldview. In fact, for me the Carrot Common became a statement about modernity's failure to address the critical issues of community, empowerment and the environment. But behind these concerns was an even more fundamental quest: a search for spiritual values that could reconnect people with themselves and with one another in a broken world.

If this is true, then it becomes critically important to understand the reasons and roots of this shift in worldview. Only by grappling with these questions can Christians begin to bring the gospel into the heart of people's need.

# THREE

# A Worldview
# Is
# Rejected

A*t the heart of phenomena like the Carrot Common lies the rejection of a* worldview that has characterized the West since the mid-1700s. This turning away from modernity has not yet achieved clarity or focus; it is still a searching process. Some of it represents a looking back to ancient ways, while other parts involve a tentative feeling ahead toward new and hopeful directions.

We are in the early stages of a cultural sea-change. And this change in consciousness sees the church as part of what must be rejected in the name of survival, hope and transformation. So if we are to speak on behalf of Christ and his church, we need to understand exactly what is being rejected—and we need to discern the signs of the times, the markers of the current worldview shift.

## Roots of Rejection

An important step in understanding how Christians might respond to the current worldview shift is uncovering some of its underlying causes. They are rooted in social and intellectual transformations that occurred during the emergence of the scientific revolution and the Enlightenment.

The period from Francis Bacon into the late 1700s changed the intellectual climate of the West. Here are the roots of modernity. The modern worldview was constructed out of the intellectual genius of men like Bacon, Descartes and Newton. These three have come to be identified as an unholy trinity who transformed the Western world. Even at the early stages, they were recognized as pivotal agents of change. Jean-Jacques Rousseau, in the *First Discourse,* said: "Bacon, Descartes, Newton, these preceptors of the human race had [no teachers] themselves; indeed, what guides would have led them as far as their vast genius carried them?"

Reflecting on the period, Kant summarized it as emancipation from all that controlled human life apart from the mind's rational capacity to know and the will's capacity to make and control. This was a period when humanity felt itself set free from the arbitrary control of the irrational, myth and superstition, the domination of external authority. Autonomy was the goal and meaning of human identity. It was seen most clearly in the instrumental rationality of the new scientific methodologies. These were used to control and make understandable the external world. The scientific discoveries of Copernicus, Galileo, Newton and a host of others radically changed our understanding of the world. Bacon, Descartes and Locke built upon these changes and gave us concepts of knowledge that undermined the old assumptions of revealed truths. Knowledge came to be based on the universal premise of observation and the systematic, empirical and rational investigation of experience. No statements were to be taken for granted a priori.

A different understanding of nature appeared with the changed concept of knowledge. No longer a receptive listening to nature as it spoke to us, knowledge was now to be gained by human beings' calling nature before the court of reason to uncover its secrets through a process of investigation. Knowledge was no longer something given to humanity from the outside; it was imposed on the world through the categories and powers of the human mind. According to the Enlightenment and post-Enlightenment assumptions, meaning comes from the autonomous human and is placed on nature. Nature is forced to yield up its secrets to the active mind.

There was in this movement a great optimism about human development and progress; the philosophers came to see humankind as empowered with the skill to control its destiny over against all that had been perceived as external, controlling and threatening—not the least of which were nature and religion. The doors of nature were stormed and battered down. Nature was to be compelled to reveal its secrets for human ends. This empiricism took away the sense of mystery; nature was disenchanted. The idea of God was less important in defining nature, except as some general initiator of creation.

This does not mean that the Enlightenment was thoroughly antireligious. Many of its exponents, in fact, were deeply religious. Its force and direction, nevertheless, are best summarized in the opening statement from Alexander Pope's *Essay on Man:* "The proper study of mankind is man."

Francis Bacon (1561-1626), who lived at the beginning of this period, was one of the initiators of the scientific revolution. The issue for Bacon, as for many Enlightenment thinkers, was knowledge and control. The senses and the imagination were deemed unreliable means for gaining knowledge of the natural world. But the application of rational categories to observation, induction and experimentation would open up what had been hidden in nature. Such knowledge was power. This was the beginning of what came to be called instrumental rationality: knowledge as domination over a nature that had been too uncontrolled, too unpredictable. Instrumental reason understands nature's function as serving human development.

Thus the sacred structure of knowledge grounded in the order of God began to be dismantled, however unintentionally. With the ascent of instrumental reason, nature no longer had significance in and of itself, or in relation to its Creator, but only in reference to human utility. It became raw material for human ends.

So the autonomous rational mind was to wield technological power over a world that had to be controlled. Perhaps the most potent metaphor for this process is the end toward which it moved—the awesome technological and scientific knowledge concentrated in the ability to smash tiny, subatomic matter. Particles are hurled at each other with astonishing speed and force in order to penetrate the secrets of the microworld. Here is the immense tension and paradox which this scientific revolution set in motion. From this compelling of nature to yield its secrets we have received both great benefits and the terrible threat of nuclear annihilation.

René Descartes (1596-1650) was, like Bacon, concerned with the certainty of knowledge. This meant a drive to discover certain, trustworthy knowledge. For Descartes sense perception was an unreliable form whereas true knowledge had to be certain. There is no way of knowing, on the basis of the senses, if things are really what they appear to be. Therefore, true knowledge was to be gained through the rational application of reason without reference to the senses. In this way the senses, as a primary source of knowledge, came to be mistrusted and seen as distinct from reason. Descartes's methodological tool for achieving this goal was mathematics— the abstract quantification of nature through numbers. Thus the primary method of gaining true knowledge of the world was through the rational constructs produced by the mind of the knower rather than a reliance upon sense perception.

Descartes divided reality into two parts. *Res extensa* comprised the material world, all matter extended in space and external to the mind. This was the object of sense perception and as such was unreliable and transitory. *Res cogitans* was the world of reliable and permanent knowledge gained through the rational categories of the mind. This Cartesian dualism of mind and matter, reason and sense perception, became an important paradigm for knowing and shaped the emerging scientific methodology.

Descartes's invention of analytic geometry, for example, became one of the primary tools used by Newton in his scientific study of the universe.

The Cartesian worldview had far-reaching implications. First, as a dualistic perspective, it separated the human thinker from the material world. It defined the human primarily in terms of mind, rationality and control while viewing nature as essentially inert matter. Such a worldview has shaped modernity, and it is now seen as a fundamentally alienating force in Western culture.

One can almost picture Descartes's person as having a monstrous head that sits awkwardly atop a body only half its size. The brain and its rational powers dominate; this is what gives the human identity and definition. The senses, atrophied, are hidden, pushed aside like embarrassing relatives; they are considered of little use for any genuine engagement with truth. Indeed, *cogito ergo sum*—"I think, therefore I am." The Cartesian model reinforced Bacon's scientific method with its utilitarian nature controlled by autonomous human beings.

Isaac Newton (1642-1727) expanded what Bacon and Descartes had developed and completed the structure of post-Enlightenment modernity through the genius of his massive synthesis—a series of mechanical laws explaining the movements of all objects. Newton's laws effectively explained and predicted how the universe worked. His synthesis was a brilliant model of a mind using mathematics to describe a passive, inert, mechanical world made up of tiny, invisible particles separated by empty space. Newton acted out a new way of knowing in which the human stood independent of nature and imposed his categories of truth and order upon it for his own ends.

But this worldview and its understanding of science are now being questioned and rejected. The growing disenchantment stems from the conviction that today's alienation and other problems are neither incidental nor avoidable results of a worldview based on autonomous, instrumental rationality; rather, they are rooted in the presuppositions of such a worldview. Versions of this critique have been presented by a broad range of thinkers—including some within the Christian tradition.

Colin Gunton, professor of systematic theology at King's College, London, says that the modern worldview has alienated people at basic levels of existence.[1] He traces the roots of this alienation to the Enlightenment, documenting how the movement's quest for intellectual autonomy affected our understanding of reality. For him the theories of perception developed by men like Descartes, Locke, Hume and Kant have effectively separated human beings from the natural order. So Western thought pictures the senses as passively receiving data from an outside nature while an active intelligence within the person gives its own shape and meaning to that perception. Gunton says that this sense of human autonomy, in which the mind, to use Kant's language, imposes its own concepts and ordering upon the "manifold" of experience, is central to the modern experience of alienation.

Technology and science have become the central realities of the modern era. The Western worldview, originally *theonomous* (seeing everything as directed by God and filled with his presence), changed over the relatively brief span of three and a half centuries, until it became dominated by philosophical materialism, in which reality was explainable in terms of human rationality and empirical methodology. There was no longer any need for the idea of God.

The result is a materialistic and almost mechanical view of human nature. Religion and "care of the soul" were largely replaced by technique—the methods of psychoanalysis and other scientifically based processes. So our modern worldview, while giving us great knowledge and power over the material world, has taken from us any adequate sense of the human self. Our "center" has been removed; the self has disappeared. In the language of Heidegger, we have created a desolate, empty picture of being. Human life has become weightless, disconnected from any point of meaning beyond itself.

There is, then, a strange paradox in the Western worldview: it can provide us with all the material goods that humankind has ever imagined;

yet it provides those goods to its own creation, an empty being bereft of soul. Here is the crisis of human existence in the West, a crisis that is experienced with deepening anxiety. While the pragmatic "if-it-works-do-it" mentality is still common in the culture, people are recognizing not just its limits but, more significantly, its potential to destroy both human and nonhuman life.

Lesslie Newbigin reflects on this dichotomizing process.[2] He describes a division between fact and value that parallels the separation between outer and inner reality described earlier by Gunton. In the West facts are public, while values are private. Facts can be observed and tested empirically; they refer to what "is." On the other hand, values refer to what "ought to be," and thus they belong to the arena of personal choice. Fact is understood to be truth, while value refers to preference. Facts are either right or wrong in the sense that they can be subject to the verification principle. Values are neither right nor wrong, but represent preferences. This implies that ethics lies not in the realm of truth but in the realm of choice, will and action. And implicit in this viewpoint is the conviction that truth and fact are the function of scientific methodology, while values and preferences are the function of religion.

It's important to recognize that such a worldview does two things. In the first place it separates inner and outer reality, so that we are severed from the world and nature. We saw this illustrated in Descartes's philosophy. And the result is not only the alienation of modern life but also the ecological crisis created by the objectification of nature. In the second place— and this for Newbigin is the essential point—it implies an *abandonment of teleology*. This means that the world is to be understood in terms of networks of causes and effects that can be determined, but the idea of purpose or final end is removed from the equation. Therefore we are lost, living in a world without purpose.

For the late Canadian philosopher George Grant, modernity represented a distinctive account of what it means to know and to make as human beings. It was moved by a belief that the mastery of nature would lead to the overcoming of hunger and labor, and to a world in which all are free. But, he says,

> progress is a more complex matter than was envisaged by those who had believed that a better society would arise ineluctably from technology. In the past human beings have been responsible for the destruction of all the members of some other species; but today when we watch the osprey's glory in the ocean storm, there is not only the awareness that this beauty may be passing away, because the eggs of the birds are being sterilized by our use of chemicals, but also that the source of life itself may become no longer a home of life. Our novelty lies in the fact that where Plato warned clearly against the dirtying of the waters, he did not face their pollution as a possibility in the immediate future. We are now faced with the easily calculable crises (concerning population resources, pollution, etc.) which have been consequent upon the very drive to mastery itself.[3]

This drive to gain mastery over nature is, for more and more people, a prime reason for the need to reject the worldview of modernity.

## The Need for Connectedness

One sign of this rejection is an emphasis on connectedness or interrelatedness. The word that keeps emerging is *wholeness*. In the case of Carrot Common, the development of a cooperative food store and credit union indicates a need for connectedness in the face of social fragmentation. The offering of natural foods reflects a longing to be reconnected with nature.

Many sensitive people today feel a lack of unity with nature, with others and within themselves. "Discontinuity and fragmentation are part of the deep structure of modern culture," O. B. Hardison says.[4] We move through a collage of identities as we function in different contexts. Most of those contexts have no connection with one another. So we begin to feel like fragments, picking and choosing styles and personas to fit differing contexts and relationships. This is not an intentional practice, as if we were bent upon deceiving people or putting on a front; it represents the complex nature of modern life.

It is hard to be an integrated person in the modern world. We seem to be forever in a process of trying to find our identity, putting together one persona and then discarding it to try another. The self-help and identity books currently filling bookstores offer various explanations for our fragmentation, whether codependence or eating disorders or some strange modern disease to which yuppies are especially prone. We read these books in the desperate hope of finding a way back toward integration and wholeness.

As we watch television our sense of fragmentation is exacerbated, for a character in a TV drama will move through a wide variety of disparate, unrelated events and experiences in a very brief period of time. Rock videos are the most extreme examples. The performer, in less than three minutes, will move through a quick succession of changes involving not only locale and clothes but also character and identity. The single, individual identity disappears into a swirling montage of discontinuous fragments.

Other examples abound. Work is increasingly distanced from home, as we commute ever greater distances to earn a living. Rapid obsolescence built into cars, computers and other manufactured products breeds a sense of discontinuity: everything is temporary and discardable.

The search for connectedness or interrelatedness is a reaction to fragmented patterns of living. People are turning to yoga, Eastern massage and holistic health centers for an experience of integration and wholeness. These are attempts to get past image to core reality.

Many people are looking for relationships that promise substance and permanence, because they have come to feel lost in the illusions of modern life. The wish to "cocoon"—to create a small, safe universe at home—and the baby boomers' rediscovery of parenting are further indicators of this search. People no longer want to experiment with styles and images. For many, cocooning is a state of mind that goes far beyond the desire to eat at home and watch videos with the kids. It is a cultural move toward self-preservation, the most recognizable way in which the culture is hunkering down to save its sense of self in a very confusing world where the landmarks are shifting too rapidly.

At another level, the elevation of earth-rooted spiritualities expresses a desire to be reconnected with nature, to know an organic rather than a mechanistic cosmos. Many are rediscovering premodern cultures and calling back their spiritualities in the belief that somewhere, outside of the modern world, there lie clues as to how we may reconnect with the larger world and enter again into its mystery and integrity. The anthropomorphizing of nature that is prevalent in advertising further signifies this search. Bell Telephone sells human communication through the eerie call of the loon, the howl of wolves across a silent, barren land or the haunting calls of whales. We want human communication to be living, organic and whole, like nature.

Nature has all but disappeared from urban, technological life; it has been replaced by an almost completely human-created reality. We have become a culture of facts and high-tech machines, and the sacramental mystery that inheres beyond the world of machine has been largely lost to us. But we long to reconnect with nature. We are moving away from individualism to interconnectedness.

We may not have the immensity of mind found in a Stephen Hawking nor an appreciation of all that the new physics proposes about the strange nature of reality, but in small, stumbling and deeply longing ways we echo the search Hawking describes in *A Brief History of Time*: we want to find some unified theory that connects and explains everything in the universe. At least we want some intimations of such a unifying whole.

There is a search for ways to resacralize nature. Part of what lies behind the reemergence of native spiritualities, Wicca worship and the use of crystals as means of garnering spiritual power is the desire to see nature as alive and, therefore, something with which we can have a relationship. Catholic theologian Thomas Berry muses, "We seldom notice how much we have lost contact with the revelation of the divine in nature."[5] This is a call to rediscover the sacred dimension of the earth itself. So for many, ecological activism is a religious quest. There is a need to experience the universe not primarily as a physical-material thing but as a spiritual reality which addresses us and with which we are connected spiritually. Where the Enlightenment desacralized the heavens, society and nature are now becoming the new domains of the sacred.

In modern cultures small, close-knit communities have largely disappeared. Only with difficulty are we able to see ourselves as interrelated with others in a common sense of belonging. Even the bonds of marriage are often expressed in the contractual language of individuals rather than the covenantal language of a larger belonging. But we are witnessing a movement back toward the recovery of a deeply communal sense of life. And this goes far beyond interpersonal relationships, reaching toward the hope of healing the estrangement between humankind and nature and creating a renewed integration with the ecosystem.

## The Elevation of Intuition

We are witnessing a shift from the primacy of the rational to that of the intuitive, the feeling and the imaginative. The priority of rational ways of knowing is linked with the quest for technological control over nature. Following Bacon, our culture has long assumed that science and technology would give humankind control over nature. And indeed we have achieved a remarkable degree of freedom from scarcity. We have learned to minimize the effects of natural disasters, though we haven't succeeded in preventing disasters altogether.

But the people who shop at Carrot Common, and many other people across North America, believe that this dream of rational control has become a nightmare. It has not brought light but has unleashed new, unforeseen powers of darkness. Consequently, we see a searching after other ways of knowing, other means of experiencing a relationship with the world. While Eastern meditative techniques are one example of this search, there are other, more common examples of this shift from a primarily rational, cognitive approach to a more intuitive, experiential approach to knowing.

To explain this change in perspective, I often compare how automobiles are sold today with how they were sold thirty years ago. Early in the age of television, when I was a young boy, TV ads would show a man, dressed in a suit, standing beside a solid, respectable new automobile. His smiling family would be carefully posed inside. The commercial would emphasize the solid, well-made characteristics of the car—all the logical reasons it made good sense to buy this make of car rather than some other. Almost the whole appeal was to the functional rationality and common sense of the prospective purchaser. There was a worldview behind that commercial.

One recent car commercial stands out as an excellent example of the changes that have occurred in our culture since I was a boy. In this commercial, set in what looks like Big Sur, California, the camera shows a ribbon of highway running along a mountainous coastline. There is no voice-over in this commercial, only music—the lilting violins and woodwinds of a Vivaldi-like piece. Toward the end of the commercial, a car drives by and the name of the automaker appears on the bottom of the screen.

The car seems almost an afterthought—but of course it isn't. What is being communicated is *an experience*. The advertisers know something that is essential for communication today: people are making decisions—coming to know how they ought to act or decide—through the intuitive, the affective, the experiential.

This is what lies behind the interest in yoga, crystals and workshops on how to gain a deeper understanding of the self and the world. People are looking beyond the rational for alternative ways of knowing truth.

## Rejection of a Materialistic Worldview

People in the West are rejecting the materialistic perspective that has prevailed for many decades. This is not a rejection of materialism in the narrow sense of being affluent and having many things. Rather, it is a rejection of materialism as the primary explanation of reality.

Materialism operates on the dichotomy between fact and value, truth and experience. It presupposes that there is nothing to know beyond that which rational categories and empirical methodology give to us. Everything else is subjective, personal experience. In its most rigid form it asserts that only the material—that is, only those things that we can see, taste, touch and hear—are real; all else is illusion. What we are witnessing is an attempt to experience life from a broader perspective than philosophical materialism can provide. Reconnecting with nature, the search for new levels of consciousness, alternative spiritualities and fresh ways of building community all reflect this shift in perspective.

The new-old syncretistic philosophies and spiritualities reject significant aspects of the Western worldview. People are less and less convinced that the world that has been bequeathed to them by empiricism and technique is a satisfying explanation for their experience. Rather than a world composed of mechanisms and disparate parts, they crave holism.

Addressing this shift, the Big Carrot's aim to sell the best-quality food is a rejection of what its owners believe Western technology has done to our food system. The development of a work environment that harks back to nineteenth-century utopian socialism is a critique of the alienation and powerlessness that characterize the typical urban working environment. The investing of crystals with metaphysical powers, the use of mantras, yoga, shiatsu and submission to gurus manifest the search for connection and spiritual wholeness in a seemingly barren environment. The attempt to make the world a better place is a bid at change from *outside* the traditional belief systems of our culture, and constitutes a challenge to that culture. More and more, people believe that only by breaking with key elements of Western thought and its sacred truths can we bring about the kind of changes that are necessary for survival.

In an exploration of the Rajneeshpuram community in Madras, Oregon, journalist Frances Fitzgerald describes its meaning for the larger culture in terms of transformation.[6] Those who became devotees of Bhagwan Shree

Rajneesh at Rajneeshpuram rejected a great deal in the name of transformation. They took new names, discarded Western clothing for orange robes and, by joining the community, left their past for a very different future. The majority of those joining this movement were university educated and dreamed of building a new world.

Such movements are not unique in Western history. There have been many attempts to create communities of transformation that sought to build a new society in the midst of the old. What is significant for cultural transformation is that today's movements are composed almost totally of well-educated, middle-class men and women who already have a stake in the dominant culture and have used its values to achieve status. They are rejecting that value system in the hope of finding something different.

A significant aspect of this worldview rejection lies in the fact that spiritual resources are sought from the East or from neopagan spiritualities, not from the Western Christian tradition. John Naisbitt writes about the shift from mainline churches to fringe and alternative spiritualities: the greatest growth in religious membership has been outside the mainline denominations, with Eastern religious groups leading the way.[7] But there has also been a renewal of pre-Christian spiritualities. Wicca and similar neopagan spiritualities are seen as offering fresh hope for the survival and transformation of human life on a threatened planet. Neopaganism is not being embraced by huge numbers of people, but it represents an important sign of change in the culture and underlines the overall theme of rejection. People feel dissatisfied with the values and culture of traditional Christianity, and so they turn back toward older traditions that "reenchant" nature with a spiritual dimension.

## Silent Assumptions

The struggle for the hearts and minds of people in the West is no longer between Christianity and materialism, or the gospel and secular humanism, but between Christianity and spiritualities that are neopagan and Eastern. Christianity, according to its most recent critics, is simply a barren "spiritual" subset of a bankrupt worldview.

This is not the only reason for a turning away from Christianity. Modernity communicated the view that Christianity belonged to a premodern era of myth and superstition. Therefore, people did not accept it into their expectations of progress toward a better "this-worldly" future. There is also a sense that Christianity has been disproved and therefore is not a tenable meaning system. But the major problem is that many people identify Christianity with the crises and failures besetting modernity. Therefore, it is not perceived to have answers for our future.

Wherever we look in the world of modernity, the church struggles to redefine its place in a culture that appears to have dismissed it as irrelevant. In Canada at the beginning of this century, some 14 percent of the population would have identified itself as evangelical. By the mid-1980s that percentage had shrunk to 7, and estimates are that by the end of this decade, if present trends continue, under 4 percent of Canada's people will identify themselves as evangelical. In 1926 some 16.5 percent of the population regularly attended church services in one of the major denominations; by 1985 that figure was down to 9.5 percent.

The statistics are no more encouraging in other parts of the modern world. In Australia church attendance has diminished from approximately 44 percent of the population in 1950 to 24 percent by 1984. In the United Kingdom between 1979 and 1989, the churches were losing members at the rate of one thousand per week. Only 6 percent of England's people regularly attend worship; there are now more Muslims in the United Kingdom than Baptists and Methodists combined.[8] In Europe the figures are even worse, with attendance rates in urban centers down in the 4-to-6-percent range. As a new Europe emerges, the churches seem to have been left out of the picture.

Christians are waking up to the fact that this is no longer our world. Once the main highway of culture, we have become a graveled back road along which fewer people are choosing to travel. But studies indicate that people are not becoming less religious. Religious belief remains high, but organized religion is less and less a viable option. There is a rejection of the church's life, a marginalization of its place in culture.

In the United States, polls continue to show high levels of church attendance. During the eighties church membership remained in the low 60-percentile range—dramatically different from Europe and Canada. Levels of commitment to regular prayer and basic orthodox beliefs, like the divinity of Jesus, continue high. Secularization in the United States is not expressed as it is in other parts of the modern world.

It is important to recognize that secularization is not a matter of belief. Belief can and does remain high in some contexts where secularization has reshaped a people's basic identity. In secularized societies people may still register high levels of belief in basic, orthodox tenets of faith. However, such belief makes no tangible difference in the way people live or view the world, as poll after poll reveals.

Thus it is quite possible to have a highly secularized society and, at the same time, significantly high levels of commitment to orthodox beliefs. In the United States this form of secularization is apparent in the degree to which religious belief has been *subjectivized.* In other words, religion is excluded from public life and focused on the personal life of individual choice. Religion is what a person chooses in order to deal with personal problems. Its emphasis is the emotional or psychological life of the individual; this kind of religion is intended to give existential meaning to personal and relational life and has little to do with the concrete realities with which the politician, scientist or social scientist would deal.

Even when conservative U.S. Christians enter the political arena, they tend to focus on personal morality. Groups like the Moral Majority saw their task as winning America back from secular humanism and liberal intellectuals—who, in their estimation, had brought about America's malaise. But these Christians concentrated their concern on issues such as abortion, homosexuality and protecting the family.

The effects of the secularization process are quite evident in one Midwestern congregation whose worship services are attended by some twelve thousand people on any given weekend. The "seeker-sensitive services" are exceptionally well planned to attract outsiders. The sermons are well craft-ed and filled with personal illustrations. The content of these services focuses upon the emotional and psychological development of the indi-vidual. One series of sermons used the Twelve Steps program of Alcoholics Anonymous to show people how they could personally grow in the Chris-tian life.

In essence, then, religion in America remains strong because it has adapted to the processes of secularization. Religion has been redirected into the private sphere of individualized choice, where inner piety and personal growth become the only criteria of religious life.

Clearly, in Europe secularization has taken a different course. Theolo-gian Anna Marie Aagaard, reflecting on the rejection of Christianity in her own country, Denmark, offered this observation:

The No to the Christian faith becomes different from the No's that Europeans have been accustomed to during modernity's history of sec-ularization. Churches and individual believers may not have been too successful in dealing with rationality's No to transcendence, but succes-sive mission endeavors and a continuous theological struggle have at least found some ways to communicate the gospel as good news to secularized men and women. Mission in the 1990's in Europe will, however, encounter more and more of the No's that are not secular, but a religious affirmation of a different transcendence, an Ultimate that looks a whole lot different from the God of the crucified and resurrected Christ.[9]

This rejection of Christianity, whether in the U.S. or the European form, is not predominantly rational. While not irrational, it occurs at levels other than the cognitive. It is experienced more than thought, felt more than reasoned. It is a silent assumption, difficult to articulate, yet nevertheless undergirding the manifold forms of its expression, whether channeling, crystals, yoga, meditation, the buying of health food or a workers' coop-erative.

## Creation Groans

Instead of assuming that the Carrot Common, with its assortment of stores and alternative values, represents just an offbeat trend, I have come to see it as an illustration of what the apostle Paul meant when he spoke of all creation "groaning in travail" as it waits to witness God's redemption (Rom 8:22 RSV). In other words, what we are seeing behind these movements is a groaning of the culture, a travail of soul in an environment that has failed to provide a life-giving meaning system and is in the process of self-destruction. The groaning is expressed in a search for new spiritualities because the fabric of the culture seems torn. There is a palpable hunger for some form of transformation, some way of reconnecting with an objectified nature, which will lead people out of the descending darkness of a failed worldview. So these expressions of transformation and hope, while critically flawed, need not so much to be attacked as to be heard as a cry of revolt, a sigh of anguish, a longing for redemption.

This motif of worldview rejection and the search for new ways to reconnect humanity with a broken nature involves the church's own life. In the following chapters the three themes of ecology, community and spirituality will be examined so that we can better understand how the church in the West has come to be seen as a part of the culture that needs to be rejected.

# FOUR

# The Church
# and Shifting
# Worldviews

T his chapter examines how the church has become identified with the post-Enlightenment worldview. I will argue that the church in the West so accommodated itself to this worldview that it is a part of what is being rejected. Three areas will be examined: ecology, community and the search for spirituality or the supernatural. Under each topic we will discuss the challenge the Western church faces if it is to address its context.

## Ecology
The overriding issue confronting modernity is our relationship to nature. One important reason the post-Enlightenment worldview is being challenged is that we have come up against the limits of nature. In the 1990s the environmental crisis is causing us to examine values that have shaped

our lives for hundreds of years. Our planet is threatened with the end of life as we know it. Sea, land and air cry out warnings of a growing tragedy, precipitated by the throw-away society of the modern West. The Exxon *Valdez*, acid rain, global warming and the diminishing ability of species to reproduce are all signs of this tragedy.

As technological progress has failed to provide a secular utopia, people's confidence in the cultural gods has been severely tested. And thus they are seriously questioning the assumptions of modernity. This questioning is evident in Earth Day celebrations and movements like Greenpeace and Friends of the Earth.

The term *ecology* has several meanings. It can refer to the human care, or lack thereof, of nature. But it also functions in a broader, even religious sense—far beyond an environmentalism that focuses on the efficient control and management of nature for human benefit. Fritjof Capra speaks of a "deeper meaning" which "recognizes that ecological balance will require profound changes in our perception of the role of human beings in the planetary system. In short, it will require a new philosophical and religious basis."[1]

Matthew Fox warns that "Mother Earth" is dying and calls for a "deep ecumenism"—an integrated, spiritual relationship with the earth.[2] Fox is suggesting something more than the personification of nature. There is a literalness in his talk of Mother Earth. Such language radically opposes the dominant Western view of nature as dead, inert matter given for human use.

For a growing number of concerned, thoughtful people, the search for new values to resolve the crisis in nature is linked with theological presuppositions that are not Christian. People wanting to heal a broken world are turning to spiritual and religious resources outside of Western Christianity. There is a belief that Christian values have contributed to the ecological crisis.

Carolyn Merchant describes a period in Western history when people did see nature as alive and sacred. This was a period before Christianity had full power and control; earth was seen as a nurturing mother to be loved and respected. Merchant argues that this was swept away when Christianity achieved hegemony in the West.[3] Anita Gordon and David Suzuki confront the "sacred truths" that have shaped our relationship with nature ever since: "nature is infinite; the biblical injunction to go forth and multiply and dominate the Earth is the human mandate . . . all nature is at our disposal."[4]

How accurate is this characterization? Jürgen Moltmann identifies three stages in the development of a Christian understanding of nature and creation.[5] The first stage, which lasted approximately through the end of the medieval period, was characterized by the attempt to define a Christian view of nature in opposition to two competing views. On the one side was pantheistic animism, which taught that nature was alive, with its own immanent mind or spirits controlling the forces of life; hence, nature was worshiped. On the other side were gnostic views which wanted to deny any living reality to nature—it was dead matter to be dismissed and from which one longed to escape. In this setting, Christian theology pointed to God as the transcendent Creator of a divinely ordered world indwelt by the Spirit and filled with God's glory and wisdom.

The second period began with the separation of nature from this Christian cosmology. As modernity emerged with its scientific materialism, any reference to God as a necessary explanation for nature was lost. Moltmann describes how this affected theological understandings of the relationship between Christian faith and nature. The doctrine of creation was reduced to a matter of personal faith; in this way, it was assumed, Christian teaching was protected from the attacks of science. Faith in creation became simply the feeling of absolute dependence: an existential truth, a statement about experience rather than objective fact.

In the modern world science and theology, Christian faith and the human understanding of the world, were shunted into two separate compartments. The result was that Christian theology took a fundamentally dualistic position to defend itself from the scientific and philosophical attacks of modernity. In both liberal and evangelical theologies, God was separated from nature and known only through an inner personal experience.

Moltmann postulates a third stage in which science and theology will reconverge to arrive at a mutual, ecologically sensitive view of the world. But that doesn't seem to be happening at the moment—quite the opposite. While science and spirituality are coming to a rapprochement, it would appear that in the popular mind Christianity is not involved in this convergence. This is not to suggest that a dialogue between Christianity and science is entirely absent. As stronger evidence is found for the Big Bang theory of the universe's origin, books and magazine articles muse all over again about God as the originator. Faith is not a spent force in the sciences. The point is where this dialogue is being taken up in the popular culture.

Much of the apparent convergence between science and religion is based on developments in the new physics, which is perceived as offering a holistic spirituality of the universe. There is not as extensive an attempt to correlate the findings of the new physics with Christianity. Physicist Fritjof Capra believes that the Cartesian-Newtonian view of nature has been nurtured and supported by the Judeo-Christian tradition. Its images of a male God who is supreme reason and absolute power, ruling from above through the imposition of laws, have been damaging, Capra says, for people have sought to emulate this understanding of the divine. He argues that the religious thrust of the old worldview was *dualistic* (God above, over, apart), and that spirituality today needs to overcome this dualism through an eclectic integration of Eastern, monistic religious philosophy with modern science. The implicit message is that Christianity cannot address the ecological crisis.

Moltmann discusses the post-Reformation debate between science and theology and how it has contributed to the present worldview rejection. From his perspective, the Reformation tended to interpret biblical material primarily in terms of *human* questions of salvation. In other words, salvation as a human, personal experience was at the heart of Reformation theology. This perspective became the normative mode of not only biblical interpretation but also Christian thinking about the relationship between faith and the world. It was also the apologetic means of maintaining the Bible's validity in an increasingly scientific world.

But one of the negative results of this apologetic focus was to cut theology off from a deeper engagement with God's created order. Instead of engaging the new scientific paradigm in dialogue over the nature of knowledge, theology came to be limited in scope to the narrow domain of the individual soul and its salvation. This salvation, for all practical purposes, came to be seen as having little to do with the world beyond the inner recesses of pious conviction, and the result was a dichotomy between human subjectivity and the so-called objective world.

Christian faith became dualistic. Its focus fell almost exclusively on the God-human relationship rather than a more unifying relationship between God, humankind and creation. What we have witnessed since the Reformation, in Moltmann's view, is Christianity's retreat from the public arena into personal faith, the inner life and piety, especially after the Enlightenment.[6] Tacitly accepting the new dualism, the church chose to stand its ground in a personal, privatized realm. The results are evident today: evangelicalism in North America is essentially private piety with little relevance to the broader issues of the day.

This goes beyond the argument between liberals and evangelicals surrounding issues of personal salvation versus social action. It is rooted in Friedrich Schleiermacher's development of a new interpretation of religion and history in his response to assaults on classical Christianity from historical studies, philosophy and the sciences. Whether liberal or evangelical, promoting social action or personal piety, today most Christians work from the basic dualism established by Schleiermacher and described by Moltmann.

Thus Western Christianity adapted to, and became a part of, the worldview shaped by the Enlightenment. The modern, scientific-technological society developed in the West, which has often been called the *Christian*

West. Thus, if many today are rejecting the post-Enlightenment worldview, then, by implication, Christianity is a part of what is being rejected. Once the arena of private piety was chosen as the proper place for religion, then, by implication, religion became irrelevant to the critical issues of public life, including the overarching issues of technology and the ecology.

The ecological crisis is leading to a questioning of the presuppositions on which scientific materialism is based. As Canadian theologian Douglas John Hall points out, the problem of modern culture's relationship to technology is more conspicuous in North America than anywhere else because "amongst us the experiment has been able to proceed virtually unimpeded, just because there were no alternative visions of society to inhibit it."[7] North Americans accepted as a given the definition of humanity developed by the Enlightenment.

> But since we have carried *that* definition to its furthest limits and have sensed something of the darkness into which it is leading us, we are driven to ask the question again. What *are* our purposes, our boundaries, our "fixed points of meaning"? We were taught to expect only light, and that it should grow ever brighter! Instead, we perceive "the terrifying darkness."[8]

One result of experiencing this darkness is the search for alternative spiritualities. People are drawing on a wide variety of traditions—but they are mostly ignoring orthodox Christianity, which is viewed as having contributed to the problem.

### The Search for Community
Community is a second underlying theme I have identified. The Carrot Common symbolizes the search for community in an environment defined by technology and individual autonomy. Jacques Ellul and George Grant argue that technology pulls community apart. They do not suggest that technology is, in itself, bad. Rather, it is rooted in the human will to power, described by Nietzsche, based in the Enlightenment's elevation of the autonomous individual.

Grant's and Ellul's concern is not machines or computers in themselves. Technology is more than a technique; it is a state of mind, a worldview. Basically they are concerned about technology as the domination of nature, and therefore of one another. As technology is wielded by autonomous individuals, it has eroded the sense of community so important to cultural identity.

The ecological crisis is one result. The bonds between human beings and the natural world are not only broken but indeed on the brink of utter dissolution. Consequently, the current search for community is broader and more inclusive than a longing for human belonging, important as this is; it is reaching out past human beings to embrace nature. It is fundamentally a search for connectedness with all of life. To miss this point is to miss the essential character of the value transformation occurring in our society.

The breaking of community is felt most pervasively in technology's most powerful creation: the modern city. The city has become a center of isolation and fragmentation. City churches are not immune to these problems; in fact, city pastors are often keenly aware of their isolation and loneliness. At a recent conference, twenty or so urban pastors gathered to discuss issues of leadership and ended up confessing to each other their sense of isolation in ministry. If this is so for our leaders how can it be anything else in our congregations?

The Carrot Common has connected two potent themes of modern anxiety. The symbol of food speaks of the ecological crisis, while the symbol of the workers' cooperative represents the search for integrative community. On both issues the church struggles.

When community and belonging are displaced by fragmentation and isolation, where does one find a theology and ecclesiology of community? What form will such a theology and church structure take in a mobile, disjunctive urban context? Where are the resources for building communities of Christian witness in a culture where life is profoundly alienating?

Historian E. R. Dodds addressed these issues in the closing section of his study of religious experience in the early centuries A.D. To explain why Christianity, a small movement among a plethora of Eastern mystery cults, should come to triumph, Dodds referred to the fact that *Christian congregations were bound together by a common life.* The church was a context of hope, care and inclusion for widows, orphans, broken and destitute people in Roman society.

The needs remain. Today's "widows" may well be single parents who are poor and struggling. The unborn, the urban poor, the immigrant populations of our cities—all these contemporary groups may easily fit into Dodds's descriptive framework. But today's church does not fit. It is making little impact on city cultures, for it has itself lost the practice of community.

The breakdown of community can be traced from the Enlightenment period and the onset of the Industrial Revolution. From the Enlightenment a new view emerged of the person. The modern came to be seen as an autonomous individual whose identity resides within the self rather than in communal relationships. We define who we are from within, not in terms of our relationships and connections. Twentieth-century existentialist writers like Jean-Paul Sartre, Albert Camus and Henry Miller evidence this understanding. Modernity no longer thinks in terms of corporateness. Many of the constitutions of modern Western democracies contain charters that define the individual as the center of reality and the prime focus of the states' concern. First we are individuals; then we choose to contract together to form relationships.

Churches have become gatherings of individuals who choose to belong or not to belong. Congregations, shaped by consumerism, emphasize psychological well-being and meeting the needs of the individual. People "shop around" to discover a church to suit their personal tastes. This is unrelieved individualism.

Evangelical doctrines of salvation augment this emphasis. Salvation is defined in terms of the individual's coming to God. Little is said about salvation as a communal event, of redemption as that which liberates us from ourselves into a new peoplehood. Preaching often underlines this individualism.

The dominant human image of modern times is the Promethean individual—a person who has, by the force of personal will, wrested control of his destiny from nature and the gods. The capitalist vision of "the self-made man" is but one expression of this pervasive motif. Another illustration of this breakdown of community and the reign of the individual is the emergence of the social service professions. Social workers are specialists hired by the state to oversee and care for society's needy, marginalized and hurting. Society pays professionals to care for its needy and broken. This brokering of life by paid professionals who have the expertise that, by implication, no one else has leaves the rest of society, which pays for the service, free to pursue its own ends and needs.

An important factor in the breakdown of community is the pluralization of society. Community requires a shared vision of the meaning and direction of life, but modernity has produced a pluralized society of divergent visions. The common language of meaning breaks down in the fragmenting explosion of choice. Increasingly, the only remaining social glue is the engine of choice itself. We have moved into a period characterized by a loss of shared experience; we are a collection of competing subcultures and interest groups, each vying for rights and place, without a common soul to hold it all together. This is not a value judgment about modern society, only a description of where modernity has brought us.

Can a morally pluralistic society remain intact when a common language of meaning and value no longer exists? Consider the polarization of today's abortion debate. The language and value structures that once held the community together have lost their meaning, so that we wonder whether real social solidarity is even possible.

Even urban planning reflects this breakdown of community. A century ago, our cities were being designed for community. There were great open parks in which people could walk and mingle, wide boulevards and buildings expressing trust and self-confidence. But the modern city is constructed around high-rise towers bristling with TV cameras and security systems that protect and control access. Contemporary architecture betrays anxiety, insecurity and the privatization of life. Still, neither Los Angeles nor Toronto is Jerusalem, and the question of what it means to build community in the modern city is very difficult to answer.

## Quest for the Supernatural

The worldview rejection I have described has certain peculiarities that deepen the problem of the church's engagement with the developing culture. Young city dwellers find the church largely irrelevant to the integrative patterns of meaning they are developing. Studies show that in Canada only 10 percent of adults in their twenties attend church.[9] Some of the reasons have just been described.[10] What is of particular concern to leaders of the church is that *this rejection is connected to a resurgence of religious interest.*

People are looking for a vision of reality that is mystical and spiritual. When 20-35 percent of North Americans claim that they have lived past lives or use channeling to receive advice from other beings, when others turn to Native American and pagan spiritualities for connection with nature and nature's spirits, then clearly there is a renewed search for the supernatural.

Why have these new searchers after spiritual reality not turned to the church? Why are new religious paradigms being sought rather than Christian orthodoxy? Part of the answer is that Western Christianity is an element of the worldview being questioned, and is viewed as irrelevant.

Over the past several decades we have witnessed the growth and renewal of cults in North American and European societies. In some ways this is not unique, for in North America there has always been a penchant for novelty in the religious scene. However, Ronald Enroth argues that when we

> look at the upsurge of new religious movements in the recent past, we must conclude that the nature of the newness in American religious experience has assumed some truly new dimensions. Religious histo-

rian Eldon G. Ernst noted that "the range of the new in contemporary American religious life and thought has moved beyond the experience of earlier generations. The movement is away from the boundaries of the Judeo-Christian heritage of Western civilization."[11]

Sociologists Rodney Stark and William Bainbridge observe that many mainline denominations have been deemphasizing traditional orthodoxy, with its focus on God's presence, and concentrated on such contemporary issues as sexuality, rights and liberation.[12] But, Harvey Cox says, those who turn to Eastern religious systems are looking for a direct experience of God and the world.[13] People want explanations of reality which allow for a resacralizing of nature. As we have seen, Christianity, in its embrace of modernity, relegated the supernatural to the inner personal experience of the pious individual.

So the culture is seeking experience that will reconnect people with the spiritual foundations of life, while many churches have been moving in quite a different direction. No wonder people have not turned to the church for meaning systems and symbols of empowerment.

The new spiritualities celebrate tradition—but mostly the traditions of premodern and non-Western religions. Dismissed as simplistic, naive and superstitious only a few short centuries ago, the ancient religions are now embraced enthusiastically.

### The Narrowing of the Supernatural

James Turner argues that the Enlightenment both demanded and forced upon Christianity a reassessment of its understanding of God. What resulted was *the rationalization of belief*.[14] Gradually the Augustinian *credo ut intellegam*, "I believe in order to understand," became the Enlightenment *intellego ut credam*, "I understand in order to believe"—a movement from belief as the ground of rationality to rationality as the ground of belief.

This shift came through a process. The birth of science and the youthful energy of Enlightenment rationalism were profoundly unsettling for the church. Church leaders began to adapt their theologies to these powerful rationalizing tendencies until belief in God came to be viewed as grounded in rationally demonstrable arguments. This was not really a consciously designed process of assimilation. Few were aware of its implications. But Turner says that unbelief spread across America during the latter half of the nineteenth century as science and rational philosophy increasingly narrowed their definitions of knowledge and had no more use of God as an explanation for observable reality.

Religious leaders responded to the revolution in knowledge by deciding that "they could best secure knowledge of God by tuning it to the dominant harmonies of the modern world."[15] Certainly, the relationship between Christianity and the emerging scientific rationalism was complex. But overall the church subsumed itself intellectually to the power of this new epistemology; few theologians noted the danger inherent in this relationship. More and more the impetus in Christian apologetics was not to question the assumptions of this rationality but to develop natural theologies in which the emerging science could be shown to support the notion of God. Theology became the stepchild of a rationality that increasingly found little use for this embarrassing relative.

This adaptation of Christian belief to the worldview of natural philosophy took a relatively short time within the span of North American intellectual history. Once the idea of God had been divided up into two modes of expression and knowing (the impersonal, mechanical guarantor behind the order of nature who establishes the natural law versus the immediate, personal God of heart religion), the supernatural was separated from nature; it was banished to the inner realm of personal experience, the arena of poetry, metaphor and mythology. The process depended on the splitting of God's role in creation, with the natural sharply separated from the supernatural. The two orders of being were pried apart from their medieval symbiosis, and the rationalizing tendencies gathered power until the supernatural came, in the West, to be identified with the unreal and the romantic.

And so spiritual realities were disconnected from the tangible realities of everyday life. God was no longer involved in the course of nature, but stood far, far beyond normal physical realities. It was left to Romantics such as Wordsworth, Transcendentalists such as Emerson, and spiritualists to find a place for the supernatural. Within Christendom, evangelical "heart religion," which placed the supernatural into the context of an inner experience of God, was fortified. Little did the evangelicals of a century ago realize that their attempts to accommodate God within the new universe of knowledge was accomplished by accepting Schleiermacher's definition of religion and the epistemological presuppositions of the emergent scientific rationalism.

## Weighed and Found Wanting

The turn toward the East is, at least in part, a judgment of the way Christianity has been coopted by modernity. In a Canadian study by sociologist Reginald Bibby, 60 percent of the respondents reported that they had had "primal experiences," some vivid encounter with spiritual forces or experiences that would not be identified as "normal." Bibby concludes that there is a pool of spiritual interest largely untapped by established religious groups in Canada.[16] In other words, the churches have little to say to these experiences.

Questioning the viability of a culture that is purely materialistic in form and content, beginning to seek a more complete and holistic picture of reality, many people are concluding that the churches have nothing substantial to offer. The new religious modes are driven not simply by inner, subjective experiences of the transcendent; rather, they represent a search for an overarching paradigm that is other than materialistic in its foundations and will reconnect people with the larger world.

The issues of the environment, community and the supernatural cannot be engaged in terms of apologetics alone. It would be wrong to assume that the religious and value transformations described thus far can be dealt with solely through solid, rational argument. Instead, the churches must rediscover their own foundations and engage in the hard discipline of understanding why the gospel came to be subsumed under the paradigm of modernity. The church must not, and indeed cannot, return to a medieval cosmology with a superstitious hierarchy of spiritual entities. Instead, we must listen to what a significant portion of the culture is saying: this creation cannot be explained purely in terms of sufficient causation; the spiritual realm is more than an elaborate mythological construct devised by primitive, prerational people. The spiritual realm is indeed real, and the supernatural will need to be seriously rethought by the church in the West if it is to recover its own roots and address the longings of people in modernity. This is an essential place of engagement.

This chapter has shown that crucial values of modernity are currently being questioned and rejected in the West. This rejection is especially apparent in the concern to halt environmental degradation, the longing for community and a search for the supernatural. The church is increasingly seen as part of the worldview that created the problems, or at least as irrelevant to the search for new directions.

How can the church free the gospel to address this situation? To answer that question we need to understand how to listen to the culture.

# How Will
## the Gospel
# Be Heard?

T oday's church finds itself in a new landscape. Until recently it held a central place in the culture, but in a pluralized and globalized world things have changed. Varieties of voices, cultures, religions and mores compete for recognition. Over the last half-century, Christianity has been progressively disestablished. Even up to the early sixties a broad-based Judeo-Christian culture informed the larger society, but since then it has broken down. Stanley Hauerwas and William Willimon describe the change in this way:

> Sometime between 1960 and 1980, an old, inadequately conceived world ended, and a fresh new one began. We do not mean to be overly dramatic. Although there are many who have not yet heard the news, it is nevertheless true: a tired old world has ended. . . . [In the past]

Church, home and state formed a national consortium that worked together to instill "Christian values.". . . . A few years ago, the two of us awoke and realized that, whether our parents were justified in believing this about the world and the Christian faith, NOBODY believed it today. . . . All sorts of Christians are waking up and realizing that it is no longer "our world."[1]

During this period what had been germinating in the depths of the culture foliated into full-blown presence, and traditional Christianity began falling like tired brown leaves shaken loose by winds of change. Today we sense the crisis of a marginalized Christianity. We have come to the end of an era; the deep roots of a churched culture have been pulled up and left along the roadside.

Church leaders who refuse to see this crisis are the proverbial blind leading the blind. South African theologian John de Gruchy concurs:

Western Europe and North America may not be going through a social crisis in the same way as South Africa is, but they are not less societies in crisis. Their crisis, which is largely the result of rapid secularisation, is . . . the collapse of values and meanings which had somehow given society its sense of cohesion in the past.[2]

We have mapped out how this crisis expresses itself in a local context, describing the affirmation of certain values and the rejection of others. Douglas John Hall speaks of "the incipient DISILLUSIONMENT of a people which has given itself long and wholeheartedly to the modern illusion."[3] As Christians, we are not observers but inextricably embedded in the process of change. We must "interpret the signs of the times" (Mt 16:3) to discover both our complicity in creating this crisis and how we can forge gospel-centered responses.

Evangelical Christians cannot stand aloof or send apologetic salvos across the bows of our adversaries' ships. We must abandon triumphalism. The church in North America has become like the proverbial emperor who wore no clothes. The crowds that once filled our churches, listening to our moralistic pronouncements, know that we have no clothes, no coinage with which to buy credence. But the challenges we are experiencing can become God's catalyst to call us into a future he has never abandoned.

This chapter will present a model of congregational empowerment as a basis for responding to today's environmental crisis, spiritual search and longing for community. But first I'd like to point out what strategies are *unlikely* to be effective.

### Ineffective Strategies

Mission and evangelism in a pluralistic society must move beyond generalized, pragmatic strategies developed in a denominational head office. The mission strategy for each congregation must, increasingly, be shaped by the values, needs and style of its context. In pluralistic cultures there are a wide variety of values which can change from neighborhood to neighborhood. The lawyers who defended the Los Angeles police offices who beat a black suspect with nightsticks understood this very well when they succeeded in changing the venue of the trial to a conservative, mostly white city. It won them their case.

Evangelism that is effective in one context may be ineffective in another. The assumptions about evangelism in a churched monoculture need to be left behind. And certain strategies will no longer work at all in our new situation.

*Church and culture as congruent.* This approach assumes that the church is an integral, formative part of the larger culture. Here the congregation continues to believe that we live in a churched culture. Evangelism strategies are based upon the conviction that the values and beliefs of the context remain congruent with those of the congregation. The primary, shaping symbols and terms of meaning (for example, "righteousness," "morality," "progress," "domination of nature") are assumed to be virtually identical. The church perceives itself as both part of and representative of the society, with an identified shaping role.

Given these perceptions, evangelism strategies look quite straightforward. In the 1950s and 1960s there was a concentration on architectural evangelism. It seemed that as soon as Christians landed in a new development, a church building, a pastor and a congregation would appear. It worked. Program evangelism aimed at youth, mothers, men, and so on responded to those who came to the church. "Construct a program and they will come" seemed to be the assumption behind strategies of mission and evangelism. There was also highly successful "biological evangelism." The young couples who flooded into the churches produced a bumper crop of babies who grew up and filled the pews.

---

**Figure 1.** Church and Culture Viewed as Congruent

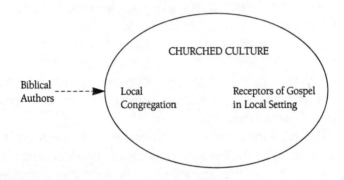

---

Yet a visit to many of these congregations today may tell a different, sobering story. The original couples are now graying empty-nesters and grandparents. Their churches are declining and out of touch with their communities. Pastors are at a loss to know what to do because they have been trained, like good generalists in a nationwide franchise, how to run a program-centered church for people who are willing to support the program. But fewer and fewer people are turning up for the program, and leaders have not been given skills to know how to respond.

Methodologies of a generation ago worked for only a limited time. New approaches to mission strategy must be developed. Above all, we need to learn how to contextualize the gospel in a pluralistic culture.

*Church renewal as mission.* In response to the crisis of decline, recent renewal theologies have sprung up. Together they represent what could be called a "church-to-church" approach.

---

**Figure 2.** Church Renewal as Mission

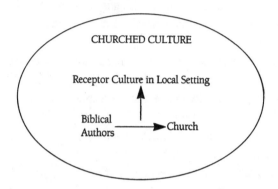

---

The conviction is that the way to recover a place in the culture is to recapture the principles of the New Testament church. At first glance this makes admirable sense. But it is interesting to observe the kinds of data these theologies extract from the early church. Book after book describes the need to renew worship, recover a biblical understanding of leadership, liberate the laity and release the spiritual gifts of God's people. These methodologies tend to address in-house matters of style and structure, arguing that they root the church back into a New Testament pattern. But they usually betray a common fault: the assumption that culture is neutral and everyone outside the church is like everyone inside the church. Thus, all the church needs to do is get its act straight and the world will beat a path to its door. But this methodology, while valuable and a step in the right direction, actually constitutes a conversation among ourselves. It does not ask serious questions about the larger culture.

## The Contextualizing Strategy

New mission strategies must be learned. Gerald Arbuckle goes so far as to say that "the chaos is so great in fact that we now must speak of 'refounding the Church itself.' " He suggests that the call to church renewal misses the immensity of the crisis. When he speaks of a refounding of the church he envisions a multidirectional process. The life of the church must be changed not only through renewed dialogue with Scripture but also, just as important, by letting Scripture speak to us through a serious dialogue with the cultural context.

The name used for this approach is *contextualization*. It recognizes the changing, pluralistic character of life today. It emphasizes the need to understand the particularity of specific contexts so that the gospel might be addressed into the situation.

Paul practiced contextualization in his missionary travels: "To the Jews I became like a Jew. . . . To those not having the law I became like one not having the law. . . . I have become all things to all men so that by all possible means I might save some" (1 Cor 9:20-22). The early church was contextual when addressing the gospel into its own diverse, pluralistic society. The task of the congregation in our present situation is to understand the cultural context, to grasp its anxieties, priorities and longings, learning to separate surface issues from the more fundamental shaping values.

In 1978 a group of evangelical scholars, under the auspices of the Lausanne Committee for World Evangelization, met at Willowbank, Bermuda, for a consultation on the relationship between the gospel and culture. The Willowbank Report summarizes their discussions. It defines the ambiguous term *culture* as the particular worldview that gives meaning to a group's reality. This worldview may be either religious (as in Christianity or animism) or secular (as in Marxism). From such a worldview come the values, judgments and traditions of a group.

But culture is never static; it is always, to a greater or lesser degree, in dynamic interaction with other cultures, being changed and reshaped by these interactions. Cultures may experience only a small degree of such dynamic interaction, or they may experience a significant amount. I diagram the "change spectrum" in figure 3.

**Figure 3.** Cultures on a Change Spectrum

| Little Interaction with Other Cultures | High Interaction with Other Cultures |
|---|---|
| Static Cultures | Accelerated-Change Cultures |
| Europe A.D. 500-800 | Native Americans After Europeanization |
| Americas Before Columbus | Contemporary North America |
| Tribal Groups in Borneo | Urbanization of African Tribes |

North American culture is far to the right on this spectrum. It is not a monoculture but a set of multiple cultures that dynamically interact and change one another.

The Willowbank Report recognized the need to take our cultural context seriously in order to establish an effective dialogue that will lead to ministry. So context becomes very important in the formation of evangelistic strategy. Awareness of the setting shapes our dialogue with Scripture as we bring the gospel to the people around us. This establishes a conversation between congregation, context and Scripture—the locus of a missionary encounter with our culture.

The contextualizing congregation must learn to "listen" and "see" where God is at work in the midst of secularism, pluralism and technological transformation. This requires the evangelist, pastor or missionary to participate in the culture at an interactive level. But it is not a relationship in which the Christian has something to give but nothing to receive—leaving the context changed but the Christian unchanged. Contextualization requires a dynamic *interaction* in which both sides are changed through dialogue.

This approach focuses our attention on the world rather than the church. It reconnects the church to its foundational purpose in mission.

## A Contextual Model

A helpful discussion of contextualization is found in Robert Schreiter's book *Constructing Local Theologies*.[4] Concerned with how the gospel may be heard in local contexts, Schreiter shows that today's cities have such a plurality and intermixing of cultures that each context is unique, with its own particular intermixing of cultural interactions. Therefore, the gospel must become specific to place and context—understandable in the language and thought-forms of each context.

This process occurs at two levels, the first of which is the broad culture. In North America this is the secularized pluralism of modernity, which is itself undergoing dramatic transformation with a good deal of testing and experimenting with alternative values and worldviews. We must understand this macrocontext in order to address people with the relevance of the gospel. Second, the transformation is being worked out in specific settings. So evangelization strategies must be of local construction. Certainly, congregations have much to learn from other churches in their settings. But the primary need is for local strategies. This is why it is so important for congregations to become skilled in listening to their own setting. Then they can construct effective local mission. And here Schreiter's model is most helpful.

According to Schreiter, we begin with the culture. Figure 4 indicates how congregations tend to do evangelism.

**Figure 4.** A Common Outreach Model

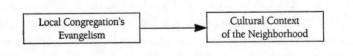

Assuming a congruence of values, beliefs and language between themselves and their setting, they move in a nondialogical, linear manner to address culture with a generalized, verbal expression of the gospel. Today such efforts bear little fruit. Figure 5 shows a more appropriate starting point.

**Figure 5.** Steps Toward Evangelism

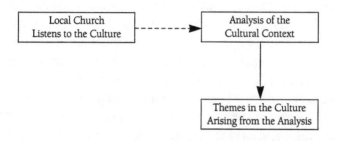

This strategy assumes a congregation has its own traditions, values and language which it must recognize. But there is a double process. Without denying its own reality, the congregation chooses to hold this valued tradition while it *listens* to the context. The dotted line in the diagram signifies this initiating willingness to hold one's own perspective in abeyance while first listening to the culture. This stops the church from proposing answers to questions that may not be primary, or even present. It guards us from imposing our assumptions on the context before the context has been heard.

This initial listening process has two parts. First, the congregation attunes its ear to what is happening. This happens through Christians' direct involvement in the context. The best way to do this is by living in the congregation's setting, joining community organizations, connecting with a broad representation of the community, learning how to ask questions and researching history, background and demographics. Above all, it's essential to be in a setting long enough to be known and to absorb its ethos—to become a part of the group the congregation wants to reach.

Clearly, the process of listening is not a technique but a way of life. It requires time, presence and a passion for both people and place. Computer printouts are no substitute for a deep, loving, listening presence.

Second, the congregation must understand the values and meanings that underlie the surface activities of the context. For example, my listening to a specific context, the neighborhood of Danforth Baptist, revealed underlying themes, particularly the dual theme of rejection and transformation. This was not obvious on the surface, yet the church would be unable to engage in a meaningful gospel encounter without grasping this dual theme. Further involvement with the context revealed three other themes within people's concerns: ecology, community and a search for the supernatural or transcendent. Finally, it became clear that those who used the Carrot Common were seeking affective, experiential ways of knowing that would reconnect people with one another and nature.

**Figure 6.** Model: An Evangelism That Listens

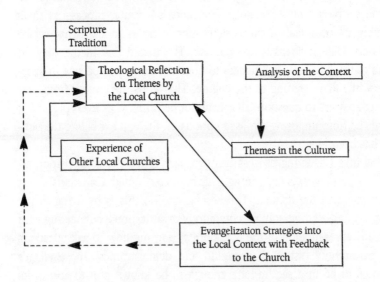

Such a listening process is a congregation's first step in understanding its context. The themes that emerge from this first stage provide the focus for the next stages of contextualization, mapped in figure 6.

In the second stage, analysis (2) and themes (3) are the basis for biblical and theological reflection by the local congregation (4). Now the congregation brings the fruit of its listening to a dialogue with Scripture. We learn to read Scripture with the eyes of our context, allowing the Bible to engage the culture and reshape the congregation's self-understanding. Strategies for evangelism grow out of this engagement, as such a gospel encounter calls for the congregation's own transformation and conversion as well as the culture's.

This methodology will be used in the next three chapters as we examine the themes of ecology, community and transcendence in order to discover strategies for evangelism. This approach requires considerable commitment to the local setting. It arises out of an incarnational theology of place in which people are more than isolated individuals with no essential relationship to their setting. Becoming immersed in a place with a people does not occur instantly but over a number of years. Perseverance and commitment are essential.

Contextualization cannot be used as simply another of the latest trends in evangelism, to be worn like a coat and discarded when the next trend arrives. It is a way of life which must penetrate into a congregation to form the air it breathes. It is an ongoing process, a spiraling dialogue requiring a commitment to change and a constant rereading of Scripture. Congregations willing to risk such a life will be at the forefront of mission in the midst of our culture.

# Ecology:
# Mind and Nature
# On a New Frontier

J*ust a few short years ago our perception of earth was changed forever when* an orbiting spacecraft sent back the first televised color pictures of our planet. Hanging in the blackness of space was a beautiful, blue-green sphere—the home we call earth. It was overwhelming in its tranquil beauty, its brightness, the wonder of its perfect symmetry.

What stranger from some distant galaxy, upon first glimpsing that sight, could ever imagine that on its surface this wondrous planet was rushing to ecological doomsday? Some experts predict that the earth of the twenty-first century will be a harsh, inhospitable place with huge deserts, drastically increased temperatures, unmanageable populations and depleted resources. These are not the forecasts of extremists, but the best estimates of cautious researchers. What is more frightening is that these predictions are not for some distant future but are already beginning to come true. The ozone layer acts like an early-warning system, registering with Richter-like alarm our abuse of the earth.

We are standing on the threshold of the greatest crisis ever to face humankind—a crisis that will radically affect the lives of our children, to say nothing of our grandchildren or future generations. A survivalist mentality grips us with anxiety over the future. The dawning awareness within our troubled consciences is that we ourselves are the creators of this terrible inheritance for our children.

Is it any wonder that people cast about for help to cope with the dark night ahead? It seems that some of the great structures created to sustain our lives have become dark powers that act with destructive force. Our panegyric to technology, our worship of our own creative powers and technical know-how, has turned into a chorus of fear as we cast about for some path that could lead us to a better destination.

The environment is the primary issue in the closing decade of this millennium. In 1989, *Omni*'s September issue had a full "Environmental Special" on saving the planet, *Scientific American* produced a special issue entitled "Managing Planet Earth," and one denominational magazine's October issue was printed on fully recycled paper and dedicated to the question "What have we done to God's earth?" These are just a few examples of how pervasive this issue has become.

Saving the planet has usurped the place of the peace movement. Environmentalism has become more than just an issue; it is the frontier for human survival.

Certainly, many people respond to the ecological crisis as if it were a fad. The Brazilian rain forest has replaced famine in Angola in the media, rock stars sing to save the trees, we learn to compost and recycle, and every other advertisement proclaims that yet another product has become "green."

Still, the situation needs to be taken seriously. In reports from the World-watch Institute, the United Nation's World Commission on Environment and Development and a growing number of world gatherings we can hear a common litany of earth's hazardous condition. Acid rain, ozone depletion, desertification, the greenhouse effect and the destruction of rain forests are some of the more obvious indicators of our crisis.

When world political leaders identify themselves as environmentalists, they show their keen awareness of how important this issue has become. In the summer of 1992 world leaders met in Brazil at a United Nations-sponsored Earth Summit. Regardless of what was or was not accomplished at that gathering, the fact that it was held indicates that the crisis is being recognized around the world.

## Rejection and Transformation: Current Responses

In earlier chapters I described a worldview shift that has two aspects: a rejection of values long held as basic truths in our culture, and a search for alternative values to transform society. This "rejection-transformation" is readily apparent in the common responses to the ecological crisis.

For many the diagnosis of the crisis is simple: The worldview by which we have lived has proved destructive. So any solution requires a worldview shift.

The problematic paradigm can be summarized briefly. Before the modern era there was no division in people's thinking between the secular and the sacred. But the development of science at the beginning of modernity created a split into two different realms. The thought processes required for moral or spiritual reasoning were seen as different and separate from those of empirical observation. *What we know* and *how we are to live*, epistemology and ethics, became separated. The natural world was explained without reference to divine action or the operations of spiritual forces. Nature was not experienced as embodying the sacred but as "dead" matter. Ceasing to be viewed as a living organism infused with meaning beyond itself, nature became a machine, a mechanism like a clock.

These changes took time. There was no malevolent intent in those who shaped this worldview. Their motives were rooted in a desire to provide a stable world. We must remember some of the trauma that these shapers of a new world had experienced over several centuries. The discoveries of Copernicus had seemed to cut human beings adrift from a secure universe of which they were the center and God was the benevolent guarantor. What was the place of humanity in this immensity of space, where our planet was a tiny presence in an unknowable universe? Nature took on a measureless, threatening enormity.

In addition, there were periods of great physical suffering. The plagues in Europe killed hundreds of thousands of people. Long, destructive wars sparked the desire to find some means of controlling irrational drives in human nature. The natural order, too, seemed an uncontrollable threat. So people longed for a measure of control and predictability. Out of these needs and longings emerged a redefinition of the relationship between humanity and nature. As we have seen nature was desacralized and objectified until it no longer was considered valuable in and of itself.

Today many thoughtful people conclude that the objectifying of nature into dead, machinelike matter to be controlled by humankind has ended in the alienation of humanity from nature. And this alienation from, and domination over, a machinelike nature has led to the ecological crisis.

The force of this analysis should not be missed. Implicit in it is the quest to replace the Cartesian-Newtonian separation between mind and body, subject and object. There is a yearning for something more than this domination by the rational—a longing for reconnection with the natural world. And many people assume that Christianity offers no answers, for it is itself deeply implicated in the ecological crisis.

### An Account of Christian Complicity

This criticism has both a historical and a philosophical basis. Historically, it is argued, the worldview we have outlined has its origin in Western Christianity. Nobel laureate Ilya Prigogine asks,

Why did the clock almost immediately become the very symbol of world order? . . . A watch is a contrivance governed by a rationality that lies outside itself, by a plan that is blindly executed by its inner workings. The clock world is a metaphor suggestive of God the Watchmaker, the rational master of a robotlike nature. At the origin of modern science, a "resonance" appears to have been set up between theological discourse and theoretical and experimental activity—a resonance that was no doubt likely to amplify and consolidate the claim that scientists were in the process of discovering the secret of the "great machine of the universe."[1]

The key word is *resonance*. It implies that Christianity was the womb that birthed the forces establishing nature as a machine. According to Prigogine, medieval Christianity insisted that the primary characteristic of God was rationality. Because humankind was created in the image of God, the primary characteristic of humanity was rationality as well. Therefore, as empirical science developed its emphasis upon observation and mathematics, it became itself proof of the supremacy of rationality. Humanity was defined as rational, standing over a nonrational natural world. The synthesis can be stated in a simple outline form:

A. God is rational.

   God is above nature.

B. Human beings are made in the image of God.

C. Therefore:

   1. Human beings are primarily rational.

   2. Human beings are, in this sense, above nature.

   3. As the image of God, human beings are created over nature.

In this synthesis scientist and theologian stood as one in their account of the natural world as senseless matter. The world does not interpret back to us what it means to be human; it is merely there to be dominated, and we can force it to reveal the truths of its shape, order and creation. In so acting upon nature, it was assumed, the scientist, the Christian thinker, was acting wholly in line with the dignity of being made in God's image. Nature was debased, while God and humankind were glorified.

This critique has a historical dimension, showing the interdependent development between Christianity and Enlightenment science. It is also philosophical, describing a view of God (as primarily rational and powerful), humanity (as primarily mind) and nature (as primarily machine, to be used and dominated). The implication is that Christianity shares responsibility for the ecological crisis.

Several other arguments need to be mentioned, though they are not as significant as the critique outlined above.

*The theme of dominion.* The Genesis 1 "dominion" text is seen as licensing the modern project of nature's mastery, domination and subjugation. Much has been written on this theme. Regardless of the text's intention, the way it has been used in the degradation of nature makes Christianity vulnerable to criticism.

*Nonhuman creation as unimportant to God.* Christians are believed to consider creation unimportant to God. This is expressed in an apocalypticism that views the natural world as a disposable piece of garbage to be incinerated at the end of time. This hardly leads to a sensitive care for creation.

*Spirituality as world-denying.* The denial of nature's place in God's redemption is also evidenced in elements of Christian spirituality. Intimacy with God has been equated with denial of and detachment from the world. Evangelicals have practiced this kind of spirituality through their pejorative use of the term *world.* Without conscious intention, such a spirituality of world denial has contributed to a worldview that excludes creation from any enduring value in the search for personal salvation.

*Salvation limited to the soul.* The evangelical view of salvation strengthens the belief that Christianity contributes to the ecological crisis. Such a view emphasizes a "spiritual" over against a physical salvation. In the language of "soul-saving" the "soul" is the nonmaterial, essential person, temporarily lodged in a material body. This "soul" becomes the object of a salvation which guarantees a spiritual body in a new creation separate from this material world. Such implicitly gnostic views strengthen the criticism of Christianity.

*Individualism.* Finally, evangelicalism betrays an unbalanced individualism. From an inadequate view of salvation has come a worldview that defines the individual as significant at the expense of everything else. This focus on the individual further strengthens the perception that Christianity has neither a theology nor a praxis to engage the crisis we face.

Christianity is becoming marginalized in part because it has become mired in a paradigm rejected by the culture. The factors I have mentioned create a perception that the gospel is irrelevant to the earth's future. Within the dynamics of rejection and transformation, the conviction is that Christianity is a part of the worldview that needs to be rejected.

## The Call for Transformation

Our discussion may be summarized in the following table.

**Table 1.** The Old Cosmology

| Human Beings (imago Dei) | Nature |
| --- | --- |
| spiritual | mechanical |
| spirit/mind | matter/body |
| rationality | irrationality |
| knowing (science) | nature as *object* to know |
| using (technology) | nature as *material* to use and discard |

Since the environmental crisis has been caused by a wrong worldview, the reasoning goes, the solution is a different worldview. Ecological theologian Thomas Berry goes as far as to propose that we put our Bibles away in order to develop a new cosmology. Paul Ehrlich and Robert Ornstein say that if we want a new world we will need a new mind.[2] If the problem is a faulty understanding of our relationship to nature, a new understanding is required.

What is being called for is nothing less than a transformation: the development of a consciousness that is unitive, holistic and liberated from the machine metaphor. What symbol will replace the machine? One model of science developed in the twentieth century represents a break with the dualistic Newtonian cosmology and is heralded as able to lead us into the promised land of a healed earth.

The source of these claims is what is called the new physics—the emergence of a whole new set of ideas concerning space and time, mind and matter. The discoveries of physics over the last century are coming to be seen as a major revolution in human thought that is forcing us to question and change our fundamental assumptions about the nature of reality.

In this revolution the long antagonism and dichotomy between science and spirituality seem to have been turned upside down. Now the material and spiritual are viewed as interrelated. And this convergence is for many a source of hope and light for the way ahead.

### The New Physics
In the new physics, the world is no longer divided into subject-object, mind-body dualisms; it is a single, holistic organism that cannot be broken into separate, autonomous parts. The notion of a detached observer is called into question, and with it the belief in a detached, objective description of the universe. Observed reality cannot be separated from the observer.

Many of our "common-sense" views of the world are being turned upside down. The belief in the autonomous, rational mind separate from nature is being shown to have no basis in reality. The natural order is something far more profound than dead matter. The distinctions between mind and matter, observer and observed, no longer hold.

Rather, the world is a sort of web of interconnections and relationships that cannot be broken down into small, independently existing units. Some experiments, like the Einstein-Podolsky-Rosen and the Bell Theorem, suggest that each event is influenced by the whole universe, and that there are instantaneous connectors to the universe as a whole. The popular illustration of this is the butterfly in a Brazilian rain forest which, by flapping its wings, causes a storm in New York City. And human beings are no longer seen as separate from nature, but as embedded in this interconnected web of relationships.

What emerges is a new way of thinking about our relationship with nature. Perhaps, many hope, these new ideas will help to heal the earth. The road toward the healing of the world more and more seems to look like a mystical, spiritual, scientific transformation of mind, away from Western, rationalistic dualism.[3]

### Gaia Theory

Several years ago James Lovelock proposed a biological theory that he called Gaia.[4] This unconventional theory views the earth as a living organism—not a planet with life on it, but a live earth. The name Gaia comes from a Greek myth about the goddess out of whom the earth was created.

Others have built upon Lovelock's speculations to argue that the earth is not dead matter, but a single self-creating being with its own consciousness. Thus mind and matter are not two separate realities but part of one single organism—earth. The human mind is itself only a part of the larger mind of Gaia.

The search for connectedness with nature is resulting in a biocentrism in which a conscious, living nature becomes the measure of all things. Human beings cease to have a unique place and are reduced to one life form among many in the evolutionary process. If Gaia theory is true, then people are expendable—especially those of the poorer nations who are more susceptible to natural disasters.

Under Gaia human domination is replaced by a biocentric domination, the rule of an impersonal nature. Major assumptions are made about the nature of reality based upon limited interpretations of quantum physics and the microworld. Questionable inferences are given great weight, and the subatomic world is made the measure of all reality. Little attempt is made to deal with the issues of conflict within nature itself; there is no addressing the nature or problem of evil nor any explanation of how individual self-consciousness could emerge from some general, impersonal consciousness.

But more important for our purposes is to recognize that we are witnessing a powerful need to reject and transform, an attempt to reconnect human life with the natural world. It fails dramatically, but the drive behind it must not be missed: a drive to discover a nondualist way of knowing in response to the overwhelming problems of ecological breakdown.

## A Christian Response

Douglas John Hall speaks about the "rebellion of nature" when he describes the ecological crisis and the culpability of North American Christianity:

> We are a people which not only conceived itself in terms of nature's mastery but also found itself the inheritor of a natural environment of immense proportions—and we have played our role on that stage unreservedly! . . .The problem of a rebelling natural world must be traced to the emergence in the Western hemisphere of a technocratic mind-set. This mind-set stems in turn from a conception of humanity which places our species "above" nature, and reduces the extrahuman creation to an objectivized status ("things").
>
> The historical question must then be put: What are the sources of such a conception of humanity and its relation to nature? . . . For many analysts in recent years have been led to the conclusion that the most decisive influence . . . has been biblical religion. . . . The ecological crisis must therefore be laid at the doorstep of the Judeo-Christian religion.[5]

Is Hall correct? Is the Bible to blame for the ravaging of nature?

We need not rush to embrace the current biocentrism. Scripture is God's revelation with much truth to show us. Perhaps the problem is that we have simply misused it and failed to develop a wholesome biblical perspective.

At times the ideas of subatomic physics and Gaia theory seem to overwhelm and undermine our faith. This new science is popularized to sound as if the truth about the nature of reality is fundamentally non-Christian. But an examination of central themes of Scripture will actually show important points of contact with this emerging paradigm. Writing of the discoveries of subatomic physics, John Biersdorf marvels that the "congruence between these new emerging world views and the central themes of the biblical witness is . . . dramatic."[6]

Many Christians rooted in biblical tradition acknowledge that we, are in the midst of a transformation in the way we think about our relationship with the natural world. Thomas F. Torrance says,

> I believe that human thought is now in the midst of one of the greatest transitions in history, which we must take with the utmost serious-ness—a transition away from cosmological and epistemological dual-isms that have had, as we now realize, a damaging effect on human culture, in science and philosophy, and not least upon religion and theology. . . . I keep asking what happens when we move from a dualist outlook to a unitary outlook.[7]

Torrance argues that, perhaps for the first time in the history of thought, Christianity is in the midst of a scientific culture that is no longer anti-thetical to spiritual reality but is operating within a nondualistic worldview not inconsistent with Christian faith.

Science is returning to the larger question of origins and worldview (often called *cosmology*). The question of God is again a part of the dialogue. But while science has moved past mechanistic dualism toward openness to spiritual connectedness, the church is only beginning to awaken to these profound changes and recognize its own immersion in the older dualities. Consequently, there persists the view that biblical faith is dualistic and of no help. Radical ecology, the new consciousness and neopaganisms constitute a smorgasbord of spiritualities and Gaia-type worldviews intended to reconnect us with nature. In the absence of a compelling biblical vision, these Pied Pipers are being followed.

We need to understand that the biblical worldview is thoroughly unitive. In the early Christian era the church formed its theology against a background of challenges from Gnosticism and Arianism. Both heresies were dualistic in their teachings regarding nature and the relationship between God and creation. In response to these challenges, the early fathers developed theologies of creation and the Incarnation which were unitary. The

Christian apologists of the day did not draw a line between the natural and the supernatural, or between nature and humankind, but between the Creator and his creatures. The formulation of a doctrine of creation ex nihilo was expressly developed to counter dualistic views.

So the resources to recover a holistic relationship to creation are present within the Scriptures and the tradition of the church. It is critical for us to remember that the worldview we have embraced for the last three hundred years is not rooted in the long tradition of Christianity.

We can begin developing a biblically unitive understanding by heeding the analysis of Lesslie Newbigin.[8] Table 2 outlines some of the modern dualities Newbigin identifies. Notice what each side is designed to represent. On the right are such items as religion and human values, while on the left is the physical world (nature), along with science and objectivity.

**Table 2.** Dualities in the Modern Worldview

| Physical World/Nature | Religion and Human Values |
| --- | --- |
| Fact | Value |
| Public | Private |
| Evidence | Choice |
| Truth | Preference |
| Science | Religion |
| Nature | God |
| Relativism | Universal Moral Laws |
| Outer | Inner |

In the modern worldview God, religion and values are private inner convictions. This dualism allows a relationship between God and the individual person, but nature, on the left side, is not part of the relational equation. Most evangelicals think and talk about the gospel and our relationship with God, but the rest of creation is missing from the conversation. It is only the God-human relationship which is perceived to have validity. In other words, we have incorporated dualism into our reading of Scripture. This dualism must be overcome.

One theological and pastoral question is key: "What is the relationship between God and humanity?" From a unitive perspective we must ask: "What is humankind, placed between God and the creation?" For that is where we have been placed, between God and the rest of creation. This results in great tension for us. On the one side, the temptation is for us to try to be like God, standing over and apart from the rest of creation. This dualism has been the road we have taken over the past three hundred years. The other temptation is in the opposite direction: to reduce the tension by identifying completely with nature. This results in biocentrism and monism. Neither the dualistic nor the monistic response is adequate. Both function out of underlying assumptions of domination—either by humankind or by nature.

The place of humanity is *between* God and creation. It is in understanding and embracing this relationship that we will move toward a healed world.

## God and Creation

The opening chapters of Genesis describe the creative work of God. Here we can learn four truths about the creation.

*The emergent creation.* First, this is a finite world with a beginning. God, the Maker, is separate from the creation. The Spirit and the Father's word bring the cosmos into being. From the beginning of the biblical material to the end, God is intensely involved in creation.

Albert Wolters makes a helpful distinction regarding the term *creation*. The opening verses of Genesis describe a creation out of nothing. But, Wolters points out, God's creative acts

in the subsequent six days of creation do presuppose an already created "earth," unformed, empty, and dark, and that the sovereign "Let there be's" of the Creator establish a variety of creational distinctions (light/darkness, above/below . . . etc.) *within* that already created but initially unfinished earthly realm. . . . Creation here has the character of *elaborating* and *completing* the unformed state of the earthly reality.[9]

In Genesis 1 we see the beginning of God's creative work as an unfolding, emerging activity rather than a series of discrete, instantaneous acts. It is an emergent creation, not fully unfolded or completed.

*A rational creation.* Second, creation requires an explanation beyond itself. We are able to pick up the expanding, distant echoes of the original explosion in which the cosmos began, and those faint sounds tell us that the universe had a beginning. What modern science has showed us is the inescapable finiteness of this universe, and therefore its contingence. This universe is not self-explanatory but an amazing, finite, rational creation, still in the process of being crafted and crying out for an explanation beyond itself. Immanentism, or any conception of the world as self-explanatory, does not take seriously the reality of creation.

*A dependent creation.* Third, Christians affirm this to be God's creation. It exists not for us but for the glory of God, and derives its meaning, purpose and direction from its Creator. Therefore, we must grasp the meaning and purpose of creation through a relationship with the Creator. The relationship we have with creation must come from our understanding of the meaning and purpose placed in creation by God. We are not free to use creation; it is not ours for the taking.

The universe has a beauty and rationality that go far beyond our finite minds. As we explore those depths, we must do so with humility and awe at the grandeur of the world's intelligible immensity. How could we ever have come to assume that this immense, deep rationality was ours to use for our own ends?

*The living creation.* Finally, creation is alive. It is not a dead piece of rock, but has been given life by God. But the critical question is, In what sense is it living? Gaia theory proposes that nature has its own inherent rationality and self-referent direction. This is a throwback to a Stoic worldview in which the cosmos is considered to be alive and indwelt with its own mind, or Logos, as a kind of energizing fate. The Stoics believed that all that exists is one and that the universe is a self-directed continuous whole.

Surely the cosmos is alive, but we must remember that this finite, dependent creation is alive *in relationship to its Creator.*

## A Three-Way Relationship

We now need to look at the larger meaning of the relationship between nature, humanity and God. This relationship has two complementary sides: continuity and discontinuity.[10]

*Continuity.* God formed us from the dust of the ground. So there is a fundamental unitary relationship between human beings and the rest of creation: all are made from the same common stuff. Humankind is embedded in the created world.

But because creation is emergent, unfolding toward completion, we may infer that humanity is not simply continuous with the rest of the world but that "human nature holds within itself all the lower kinds of life."[11] This is not intended to uphold any particular scientific view of creation, but rather to suggest that God created us as the essence and presence of all the created order. The God-given reality is that in our continuity with nature we carry and recapitulate the developing, emerging meaning of the creation.

This characterization of our relationship with nature gives us great dignity, yet also emphasizes the biblical truth that we are made of the earth and are not some stranded space aliens waiting for rescue. Our peculiar calling, stewarding if you will, is to express the meaning, purpose and direction God has given creation. This is our immense privilege and priestly vocation. It is an office of love, listening and servanthood. We are penetrated by all of nature; we are its voice and mind, not its master to dominate.

But even this is not sufficient. If we stopped at this point of continuity we would end up walking all the way down the road with those who affirm a Gaia-type monistic universe. Scripture describes our relationship not only in terms of continuity but also in the language of discontinuity.

*Discontinuity.* The discontinuity inheres in the fact that unlike the rest of creation, we are made in the image of God. The Bible gives us a unique place within creation. We bear the image of God, the imago Dei. In Scripture the imago Dei refers to the meaning of humanness and is a relational or communal term. It operates in a double, connected way: humanity is related to God as Creator and to the larger created order (in a relationship often referred to as *stewardship*). In other words, *relationship* defines the meaning of the image of God, whether this be the God-human, human-creation or human-human relationship. The imago Dei is expressed relationally at all these levels, and they interpenetrate one another. Terms like *dominion* and *stewardship* must be interpreted through this relational context. Dominion is dependent upon the imago Dei for its meaning.

How should humans relate to the rest of the created order? The Bible describes us as being created to have a kind of lordship over the earth. We are to be God's viceroys in creation. But the meaning of that regency is derivative from God as Creator. Lordship, or stewardship, is not separable from our relationship with the Creator. Thus we see how important the unitive God-world-humankind perspective is. The one cannot be rightly understood without relationship to the other. "The inseparable trio is Creator-Man-Creation, man being the participant mediator between Creator and Creation."[12]

The dualistic problem of our modern period has been that on the secular side only two elements have been taken into account—namely, world and humankind; and from the religious, or Christian, side, only two elements have been taken into account—God and humanity. All three must be treated as an inseparable unity.

God has begun a great work of creation. Humanity is an integral, inseparable part of this contingent, variegated creation. But even more wonderful, God has put his image in humankind and called us to the task of completing the work of creation. In this sense we are the mind of creation. We express its fundamental rationality. As priests of God, the Creator, in a great act of worship and completion of our God-given vocation we enter joyfully into the mystery and immensity of this universe, to discover and unfold and express its rationality and beauty. In doing so we are truly cocreators with God, praising, like St. Francis, the unfolding mystery of this created order of which we are the most sublime expression.

*Christ the Redeemer of all creation.* Creation is contingent; the Creator is utterly separate and different from the creation. But throughout Scripture, and supremely in the Incarnation, God is intimately and continually involved in the life of the creation. The Christian goes beyond the discoveries of physics to understanding that all things are being made one through Christ the incarnate, redeeming Cosmic Lord.

Scripture is clear that creation and redemption occur uniquely in Jesus Christ. Christ is creation's Lord and Redeemer. This is expressed in the New Testament by the confession that "in Christ" all things "consist" or are held together (Col 1:15-23). Therefore creation is one undivided whole not in itself but in Christ, its preexistent Lord.

Through the Fall, this unitiveness was torn asunder. But echoes and images of unity remain, and intimations linger. The unity can be sensed deep within the created rationality of the world, but its meaning and explanation are clouded.

But Christ's redemption is intended to restore the broken, marred unitiveness of the whole creation. Thus the basic intuition of wholeness which is being recovered by science and expressed by ecologists and Gaia theorists is correct. The longing for a restored, unified creation is also biblical and right. But such restoration will not come from within the system.

What a tragedy that our culture seems no longer able to recognize that its longings to know a healed world are fulfilled in Christ—what a sad commentary on the church's dualistic accommodation, our profound failure to obey Scripture. But what an opportunity we have today if we can only recover a biblical understanding of the full redemption Christ has brought to the world.

Romans 8:18-25 describes a created order bursting with anticipation and longing because the salvation of human beings in Christ is to release and redeem the nonhuman creation. Here is our priesthood. Redemption is cosmic, for the whole creation. It is not limited to individuals. Christ intends the restoration of all things into wholeness in himself.

The implications are immense. We are so much a part of the created order that our redemption is to bring about the release and redemption of the whole created order. This is so much bigger than salvation for individual disembodied souls. This is life for our world! How could we ever have lost sight of so great a salvation, so wondrous a calling? We have a common destiny with the whole created order.

This is not a throwaway world, to be discarded by its Creator. As Paul marvels, the secret is out in the open. The mystery of the rationality of this creation has become manifest in the life, death and resurrection of Jesus Christ, and it is this: that all things in heaven and on earth are being brought together in their Creator, Christ himself, who died and rose again for the healing of the whole creation.

# SEVEN

# Community:
# Making the World
# Whole Again

T he Carrot Common developed as a workers' cooperative, a "common" setting where diverse interests came together to discover ways to make the world a better place. In this way it symbolizes the search for community.

The 1980s were not a high point for a sense of community in North American culture. Several retrospective books have sounded the chord on this "me-first" decade. Laurence Shames's *The Hunger for More* outlines how this decade of greed has begun to prompt a search for fresh values.[1] Barbara Ehrenreich gives a harsh indictment of the decade in *The Worst Years of Our Lives*.[2] *Harper's* magazine recently published a lead article under the caption "Enough About Rights; What About Obligations?"[3] It concluded that "the vocabulary of rights is nearly exhausted." One contributor, Mary Ann Glendon, professor of law at Harvard, observed:

For most of our history we seemed to be endowed with inexhaustible social and natural resources. Only recently, with consumer capitalism well advanced, with our heterogeneous population growing even more diverse, we have sensed that we've been consuming our social capital without replenishing it. While rights have been proliferating, we have paid little attention to the seedbeds of civic virtue from which rights derive their surest protection. Now we are beginning to sense this erosion, and it scares us.[4]

Someone has described modernity as a journey from society to self. By the late eighties self-centered individualism had reached a disturbing pitch.

But independence, individualism, mobility and success have not brought us the world we expected. The work ethic, the cult of busyness, the romance of being able to uproot ourselves and travel wherever we chose—after the excitement of this lifestyle has come the recognition of its fundamental emptiness. Fast cars and the fast track became circles in which we chased ourselves but failed to find the meaning promised at the end of the ride.

Even during the "worst" decade, the eighties, some were beginning to feel a weariness with the perpendicular pronoun and a recognition of how fragmentary the culture had become. The Carrot Common was a sign of that change, a search after values that would be more community-centered. A part of the rejection/transformation motif we have tracked is a renewed search for community. The metaphor of mobility is being replaced by that of journey. Where the former is symbolized by the solitary individual driving a powerful car down a highway toward success, the latter suggests a common direction toward a destination. *Journey* bespeaks going with others toward a particular destination. It suggests the biblical imagery of a journeying people on a quest, a purposeful direction. The journey metaphor suggests *community*.

It's becoming clear that this metaphor of journey is broader than the search for personal fulfillment; it is an emerging sense that if we are to survive, we must come together and rediscover a common identity with each other and the battered planet that supports our collective life. In the crisis of modernity, community and belonging are returning to the center of our agenda.

Joseph Campbell suggests that the theme of journey and quest is the central metaphor of all the great religions. As the eighties came to an end, Campbell's popularity soared, his books filled the stores, and suddenly, it seemed, the culture was making a sharp turn toward some kind of corporate "we." The image of the 1990s is not a strong loner like Clint Eastwood, but a corporate image, rather like Chaucer's motley band walking together along some dark and threatening trail, looking for a new Canterbury.

The search for community is a quest for values to heal a fragmented humanity. People want to come together out of their fragmentation to cooperate in the creation of a new world. There are numerous signs of this change. The rise in volunteerism and the receptivity to community recycling efforts are illustrations. Models of leadership are moving away from the individualistic heroes who, through the power of their might, change everything. Lee Iaccoca and Donald Trump have ceased to be our paradigms. Leadership is becoming participative, workplaces are being debureaucratized, hierarchies are being flattened, and worker participation has become the new rule.

In their book *The Addictive Organization* Anne Wilson Schaef and Diane Fassel used the model of a hologram to describe this paradigm shift. Everyone is seen as essentially connected to everything that is occurring within a system. The isolated individual, the heroic stereotype holding everything together, is in eclipse.[5] Barbara Killinger wrote a book called *Workaholics: The Respectable Addicts* that touched a profound chord in a culture full of people out of touch with themselves and one another. Robert Bly in *Iron John* and Sam Keen in *Fire in the Belly* addressed the loss of male identity and called men to recover it through reconnection with each other.[6]

These are all signs of the longing for change. As modernity loses its shaping influence in the culture, people are wanting a different paradigm for living together. But the shape of the search is not what we have normally identified with the idea of community.

## The Community of Transformation

The conviction that Western culture is moving through a period of fundamental *transformation* is guiding this search for community. But what does transformation have to do with community? A great deal! Community is founded on a vision of what society can become, and the language of transformation offers a vision for the future. Transformation is a community-forming image in a time when people want a fresh vision for the future.

It is not just fringe groups that herald a new future. Bestselling authors like Alvin Toffler and John Naisbitt are doing it with enormous commercial success. Scientists, ecologists and social theorists argue for the need of a transforming vision if we are to survive. They tap into a hunger for hope, a desire for alternatives in the midst of fragmentation.

But a transforming vision of community is possible only among people who have a common language of meaning. Individualistic, pluralized societies have lost this common language. Christianity used to provide it, but Christian assumptions have been displaced by a multiplicity of values and norms. So we lack a vocabulary to converse about the values that shape our culture. Society has become a communicative Babel in which genuine engagement is impossible. The culture is adrift in a sea of conflicting and competing meaning systems.

At first glance, the movements and spiritualities that have emerged through the last several decades appear to be more illustrations of the problem: an array of competing groups with a wide variety of divergent meaning systems and languages. Green politics, Eastern mysticism, neo-paganism, new science, paranormal psychology, business futurists, trends specialists, the human potential movement and others proffer their own languages of meaning. Surely this diversity is an illustration of the problem.

But this is not the case. If one listens carefully, one can detect something of a common language among these disparate groups, for each describes a transformation that will launch a new future. Discontinuous languages of meaning are bringing people together around this vision of transformation.

This collection of groups represents a reconciliation of two tensions in Western culture: freedom and solidarity. How do we balance the need to be freely choosing, self-authenticating individuals with the need to belong, to be part of a common solidarity? Perhaps it is possible through a network of diverse groups offering a common language of transformation. This is the genius of a place like the Carrot Common and is a rarely recognized factor in the worldview changes that are now taking place: a range of ideologies are able to be housed under a single roof.

What makes the search for connection work among these divergent groups is their common commitment to making the world a better place, to an optimistic hope in some vaguely spiritual belief that we are in a time of monumental shift in the way the world works.

These visions of utopia are fueled by an admirable desire to transform a culture that has become destructive and alienating. I am convinced that these hopes will not stand the test of time, for they lack a strong foundation. Still, we must recognize the drive to create a future that reconnects people and the world.

### A New Symbol of Community

Symbols are potent forces in the formation of community. Think of a nation's allegiance to its flag—a symbol that overcomes differences and welds people into a common identity. A new symbol of belonging has emerged in our day: the image of earth, fragile and broken but still beautiful, suspended alone in the immense silence of space.

The search for community is forming around our fragile planet. Michael Ignatieff has put it this way: "No generation has ever understood the common nature of our fate more deeply, and out of that understanding may be born a new identification, not with this country or that, but with the earth itself. . . . Modernity is changing the locus of belonging."[7] This locus is the desire for unity with the whole natural order. The idea of Gaia, the resurgence of neopaganism and the introduction of myth into the vocabulary of community and transformation are reflections of this overarching attempt to reconnect humankind with nature and build a community beyond interpersonal relationships. This is an important insight for Christian engagement: the drive for a renewed community is global in scope.

This may not resonate with our normal idea of community. But I am convinced that the forming of a cooperative at the Carrot Common, the gathering of groups to reconnect with nature through guided imagery, the turning to the East and the embrace of monistic mysticism are all part of our culture's longing for reconnection. It is a search for community which is personal, social and world-embracing. And it includes ideas about the world which seem very strange to most Christians.

A good deal is right about this search, but there are also serious problems with its direction. The language associated with an earth-centered, holistic community is often based upon the creation of ambiguous myths. The idea of Gaia, notions of a past ecoharmony between humanity and nature, and ecofeminism's teachings concerning the developments of sexual hierarchy are, for the most part, new myths. There is also an elaboration of mythologies about the future. The language of transformation is an example. Dividing history into ages based upon notions of First, Second and Third Waves (Toffler) or the Sensate and Ideational Ages (Sorokin) and then prophesying that we are about to enter a time when we will achieve communal wholeness is mythmaking on a grand scale. It is the secular equivalent of dispensationalism.

A quick survey of a bookstore's "spirituality" and "ecology" shelves will reveal a plethora of books that offer new myths about the loss of, and the means of regaining, ecocommunity. The August 1991 issue of *Omni* contained an interview with Morris Berman, who has written several influential books on this theme of reconnectedness and community with the earth and other people. A process of mythmaking underlies Berman's ideas. He postulates a time when there was no split between self and other, when there was some form of ecocommunity in the world. But, Berman guesses, a sharp split "occurred during the Neolithic agricultural revolution (about 8000-9000 B.C.), when animals were domesticated." He tries to define differences between Paleolithic and Neolithic people, even though he acknowledges that meaningful evidence of the former has been lost in time. So his position requires the creation of a new mythology about the past.[8]

While the search for a broader experience of community is understandable, it is fueled by such mythmaking. And in this sense it is a retreat, an abandonment of the hard intellectual issues that must be addressed. Many current attempts to create some kind of global, cosmic oneness represent a giving up of struggle and responsibility to weave projections and fantasies arising from anxiety about the future. We will not have a healed future based on myths about the mystical oneness in all creation once human beings are submerged into the whole and become no more than a part of Mother Earth. We will not create community by replacing male hierarchies and domination with myths about female gentleness and goddess religion. This is a flight into irrationality, a leap into a neoromanticism that immerses us in good feelings but has neither the substance nor the ability to generate what it promises.

The current mythmaking is an ahistorical search for a new millennium. It is the rejection of the dominance of technical control in favor of the dominance of a mythologized nature. There is still a loss of the human center so central to biblical faith. Without the recovery of this center there will be no hope for a healed creation. The new mythologies cannot create the kind of community people want. What is required is something quite different, and this is where the gospel has the only word of hope.

## The Church and the Search for Community

We do have hope to offer. But first we must recognize that a church that has shaped its life around the needs and demands of the individual has sold its birthright. That is where the church in North America finds itself today. We have read the culture well and sought to service its demands. But in the new future that is struggling to be born, Christians must recover the biblical core of our identity as the people of God, the community of Christ. This recovery is central to the witness of the gospel.

We are at a point of great opportunity as God's people. In the immediate past the tide has gone out on Christianity as the language of meaning for our culture. But what initially appeared as the broad new plains of opportunity and freedom provided by pluralism and secularism is proving to be a long series of treacherous mudflats that have left people bereft of meaning and direction. And here lies the opportunity of our time. The tide is beginning to turn, moving toward the shoreline—a tide of longing and searching for a way out of the endless mudflats of dystopia and disintegration.

But this turning is fraught with uncertainty. Tides do not come in straight, and there is no simple turning back toward Christianity. People are looking for alternative shorelines. Coming in upon us is a diverse sea of faith. It carries bruised and battered individuals wanting to believe in something more than themselves, wanting a compelling vision of life's wholeness. The long ebb tide of post-Enlightenment secularism has produced a great crowd of lonely people, standing in shivering isolation on the deck of a ship that lacks both compass and tiller. But these people will not be reached by the old language of Christendom; it is no longer on their map of meaning.

We must understand where people find themselves today and address their need to experience a transformational reality. Scripture speaks of a covenant people joined together in a pilgrimage toward the wholeness and healing of creation in Christ. This transforming vision must shape our proclamation of the gospel and the reality of our lives together in congregations. The old cant of guilt, death, self-centered spirituality and the dualisms of dematerialized souls waiting in this anteroom to heaven will not touch people's longings for a new kind of earthed community. The vision of a world beyond has been displaced by the hope of a common, healed life here on earth.

The church will need to evidence a listening, incarnational life. When

Paul arrived in Athens he found a city on an endless search for God. But he did not retreat into his Jewishness, using that language system to communicate with the Athenians. Nor did he use the symbols of his Jewish context when addressing them with the news of Christ's life and power. On the contrary, Paul entered their world; he listened in order to use their language and their symbols so that the gospel would be heard. The apostle never planted communities of self-interest, but groups of Christians that could respond to the needs of their "secular" context. This is what our churches need to recover.

If the gospel is to be heard, the people of God will have to communicate a vision of transformation that is possible on a global as well as a personal level. We have been given the treasure of God, the secret of God's great purpose in Christ for the healing and transformation of the whole creation. The yearning for transformational community is precisely what the gospel is all about. Such a vision gives a community its identity. It is central to the kingdom Jesus announced. We must recover the breadth of the gospel's transforming power.[9] Hauerwas and Willimon describe this in terms of journey.

> When we are baptized, we (like the first disciples) jump on a moving train. . . . We become part of a journey that began long before we got here and shall continue long after we are gone. Too often we have conceived salvation—what God does to us in Jesus—as a purely personal decision, or a matter of finally getting our heads straight on basic beliefs, or having some inner feelings of righteousness about ourselves and God, or having our social attitudes readjusted. . . . Faith begins not in discovery but in remembrance. The story began without us, as a story of the peculiar way God is redeeming the world, a story that invites us to come forth and be saved by sharing in the work of a new people whom God has created in Israel and Jesus.[10]

The gospel provides a vision of community that is rooted in God's kingdom and the liberation of creation from the bonds of sin. This kingdom vision can transcend empty dualisms, and it can provide us with the resources to be a witnessing community.

Our culture does have the potential for a common language of meaning. This potential is evident in the desire for connectedness and transformation. The people of God have the opportunity to forge a language of meaning by recovering the scope of God's reconciling purposes in Christ.

If this is to happen, we must resist the mythologizing process discussed earlier. The adoption of nature mythologies will not lead to a new tomorrow or address the crisis of our broken world. Feeling, emotion, myth and intuition will not get us to the future we all want. The gospel repudiates the dominance of nature. In biblical faith there is no divinized, controlling nature. There is no Gaia-type spiritual center that makes "nature" an entity with its own life and power. In fact, biblical faith does the opposite. It releases human life from the control of nature in the forms of cyclic, endlessly repetitive views of history. Nature is denied a life and status of its own as a divinity that must be placated, served and appeased. Scripture abolishes fertility and goddess worship. Only in a biblical context can nature be freed to itself, and human life freed for proper, God-given stewardship and love of nature.

We need an apologetic that demonstrates that there can be no new community on earth until people are reconciled to one another and healed within themselves. This requires not a mythology about the earth but a hard look at ourselves—a clear expression of the gospel in the language of transformation and healing. God's people must not join the anxious desire to escape history or rewrite it into new myths. We must elucidate a gospel that answers the question of how we can bring about a healed creation. Then we will become menders of the broken walls, those who bind back together what has been torn apart.

Jesus Christ, the universal Lord through whom all things were made and all creation will be healed, is the hope of the world. Christ addresses a broken creation by calling human beings back to their dignity as reconciled, healed people. This redemption of men and women in Christ is the only hope for a transformed world.

## Small-Scale Community

A transformational vision of community must find expression in local contexts. The Carrot Common exemplifies this search for global community at a local level. Congregations need new wineskins true to the call to be God's people for the world.

The Carrot Common offers pointers for forming wineskins in congregations. The Common is made up of diverse groups in voluntary association to engage issues in the culture. The food co-op responds to people's environmental concern, and it provides alternative answers based upon a larger vision of change and renewal.

Small communities living out their vision in a neighborhood will be powerful community-forming groups in our culture. Churches will effectively evangelize as they form such communities centered on a world-changing vision through Jesus Christ. This goes far beyond a Sunday sermon on the theme of community; it is a lived-out incarnation of the transformation Christ brings. This incarnational involvement will mean rediscovering a Christianity more compelling than religious, therapeutic, individualistic groupings designed to meet our needs and reinforce our views.

Recently, a group of church workers in Toronto participated in a one-day conference designed to discover what God might be doing among his people in the city. Two visitors listened to the discussions and then reflected on what they had heard. One was involved in training seminarians; the other was a former mayor of the city and a well-known advocate of social change. Their reflections were troubling. One described the group as full of the weariness of well-doing, of fighting churches to see past themselves—weariness over the spiritual crisis in people and the diminished sense of the Spirit of God moving in any recognizable way. Above all, it was observed, there was no sense of belonging, of a community built around common values and visions. One telling statement was that the group was unable to speak the language of the kingdom. There was a silence around those central values, as if they were not the cords that bind God's people together.

The second observer said much the same thing. The group was described as people who felt powerless, with no sense that the systems and structures of society could be changed. He saw the church as rendered powerless by the belief that control lay in the hands of government, corporate agendas and the city's mad rush to achieve "world-class" stature. His most telling word was that he had witnessed a gathering of individuals whose only sense of solution lay in personal relationships. What concerned him most was that there was no sense of the *polis*, the power and authority of neighborhood communities to come together around a vision for the future and work toward change in the city and the world.

As these two outsiders found, today's church is not a community engaging its culture with the energy and conviction of a great vision. It is a ghettoized group of individuals who have abdicated responsibility for the larger issues of culture because they believe that the forces of government and corporate systems are too powerful to be overcome. The concerned, committed church workers of Toronto had become a reflection of the larger society they wanted to redeem in the name of Christ. They had become isolated individuals, enveloped with a sense of powerlessness, no longer believing they could effect much change. The problems seemed too big and too complex.

The vision of the church as a journeying people called to a transforming vocation extends to social structures and neighborhoods. The good news is that in Christ this polis, which has become broken and alienating, controlled by spiritual powers and impersonal systems that break and diminish human life, will be transformed into the polis of God. That is what John's great vision on Patmos leads us to: the broken cities of this world will become the city of our God, and all creation will be healed.

So we are to enter these strange Babylons—the places where we live and work—where we seem to have been taken as captives, away from the security and familiarity of our Jerusalem, our lamented past as a "Christian society." And here, in this polis that no longer seems to hear or understand our "Jerusalem" language (Ps 137), we are to put down deep roots; we are not to run away from but to love it, to seek its health and cry out for its future transformation (Jer 29:4-7). This love for the local context in all its strangeness and opposition is at the heart of the gospel community's vocation.

As we make our way in a strange land, we are to live and build and shout aloud about a journey, a people on their way to a future, a time when all will be transformed and the whole of creation healed. But we dare not resort to the old language of Christendom. We must listen, listen, listen to the heart-cries of those who are creating spiritualities that scare, offend and threaten us; then we can speak into their longings with their language.

We need a movement of God's people into neighborhoods, to live out and be the new future of Christ. It must be a movement that demonstrates how the people of God have a vision and the power to transform our world. This is not the same as current attempts to grow bigger and bigger churches that act like vacuum cleaners, sucking people out of their neighborhoods into a sort of Christian supermarket. Our culture does not need any more churches run like corporations; it needs local communities empowered by the gospel vision of a transforming Christ who addresses the needs of the context and changes the polis into a place of hope and wholeness. The corporation churches we are cloning across the land cannot birth this transformational vision, because they have no investment in context or place; they are centers of expressive individualism with a truncated gospel of personal salvation and little else. Our penchant for bigness and numerical success as the sign of God's blessing only discourages and deflects attempts to root communities of God's people deeply into neighborhoods. And until we build transformed communities there is no hope for a broken earth.

Turning again to the "wineskin" of the food co-op, we encounter an attempt to be a community of resistance out of a vision of change. The Big Carrot's founders formed a structure to resist the power of mass culture and the impersonal ethos of institutions. By modeling shared ownership and responsibility, they have sought to overcome hierarchy. Profit has not been the motivation as much as a vision of making the world a better place. Again, local values are shaped by a larger vision. This combination of local empowerment and global concern has produced an attractive image of community for those who frequent the Carrot Common.

Congregations, too, can be centers of empowerment as they identify how structures model the visions by which we live. Corporate structures and hierarchical styles of leadership that exclude certain groups speak eloquently about how we view the world and its needs. We need churches that look something like the Big Carrot food cooperative—people invested in a common cause bigger than themselves, sharing responsibility for the life and work of the community and willing to work out together the hard issues of creating and shaping community in a neighborhood. Such communities of faith can transform the culture, just as those small communities of faith spreading out across the urban centers of the ancient world turned that world upside down for Christ.

J. R. R. Tolkien's trilogy *The Lord of the Rings* tells the story of a little, comfort-loving, humanlike "hobbit" who is called to leave the security and warmth of his solid house in the ground for an incredible adventure. Middle Earth is about to be plunged into great darkness, evil is afoot and security is no longer possible. The hobbit, with a few friends, sets out on a long, perilous journey in which they become key to the salvation of all Middle Earth. They resist their calling; they feel very small and vulnerable and want to be left alone in their security. But they go. Along the way, others come to join them in their task of bearing a ring to the mountain darkness.

What strikes me about Tolkien's work is the rightness of his insights. The first book of the trilogy is titled *The Fellowship of the Ring,* and what Tolkien is telling us is that community occurred when a disparate group of creatures, some of whom had no natural love for one another, had their lives forged together around a call to a task that transcended their personal identity and need of security. They became a fellowship out in the barren wastes and on the cold mountains, not in the security of common interest groups waiting for people to come to them. The community emerged on the way as they discovered the immensity of their task, and they began to form a vision of what was happening and what could happen in Middle Earth.

There is a tide turning today; men and women are hungry to catch the wind of that kind of belonging. Would that we, God's people, would hear this wind of the Spirit blowing over our culture, for in it is the power to form such a community of Jesus Christ that the whole earth will be transformed.

# The New Spirituality: Quest for Transcendence

T *he third key element of today's change in values is the renewed search for* transcendent spiritual direction. In a sense there is nothing new in this quest, for secularism has been unable to eradicate people's inherently religious need for something beyond the material. What is different now is the nature of the search.

Polls taken in North America always show high levels of religious belief. At first glance this is comforting. We translate this into the assumption that most people still believe in just the same way as they used to, and we just have to find better ways of reaching them. We assume that what keeps people away from church is materialism and affluence. People are so busy earning a living, getting ahead and enjoying the good life that they have no time for church. Some Christians say, too, that we have created a society with low levels of commitment, so that people are not open to the high call of the gospel.

Such views assume that we live in a religious culture whose beliefs are basically the same as ours, but that distractions keep people from involvement in the church. Therefore, we need better methodologies, strategies and leadership to compete with the distractions. In other words, the problem is viewed as a mechanical or methodological issue that can be solved with pragmatic strategy and innovations.

But this is a misunderstanding of current realities, and it may account, in part, for the fact that most church growth is actually a circulation of the saints. It is true that nine out of ten North Americans believe in the existence of God or some higher being, that eight out of ten feel they will have to give account for what they have done with their lives, and that over 90 percent pray at least once per week. But does this kind of head counting really tell us what is going on?

If polltakers had returned to Israel at the time of Jeremiah, before the captivity and the destruction of the temple, they would have found equally impressive levels of belief and prayer commitment. But the prophets saw the situation differently: they recognized the development of beliefs and values diametrically opposed to the worship of God. Syncretistic religious practices had undermined the faith of Israel. The prophets knew that head counting didn't tell the whole story, nor could it lay bare the deeper levels of change in Israel.

In the same way today, in the midst of reassuring polls there are deep changes, countermovements that cannot be addressed through pragmatic technologies of communication. People do want to believe; they long for salvation. But we must grasp the shape this search for transcendence is taking.

Novelist and social critic Tom Wolfe suggests that in the decade ahead we will see a resurgence of religious interest. People are no longer considered strange or out of step if they express interest in the spiritual. *Omni* magazine gave a whole issue (August 1991) to the theme of the search for

God.[1] Matthew Fox has written a highly popular book, *The Coming of the Cosmic Christ*, that mixes Christian theology with ecospirituality and salvation through "Mother Earth." Hollywood recognizes the turn and has produced an array of movies appealing to people's need to believe in the spiritual world. Movies like *Always, Ghost, Dead Again* and *Hollywood Stories*, to name a few, capture people's sense that there is something more and we can connect with it.

Too often when Christians critique this quest for transcendence they emphasize its more bizarre manifestations: pagan rituals, witchcraft, Eastern religious practices and meditation techniques. While these are present, they are only the surface manifestations of something much deeper, and they can be viewed from another perspective. They reflect a rejection of the religious values that have shaped our culture.

## The Meaning of Transcendence

For Christians, the word *transcendence* expresses the idea that God is other than creation. But this is not what the new spiritualities mean by the term. *Transcendence* is often used as a synonym for mystical experiences of direct connection with what is perceived to be the true reality behind ordinary life. In such experiences the old dualisms of mind and body, self and others are removed. The focus of this transcendence is an experience of unity with everything else. Such experience, it is felt, is not available to us through the traditional ways of knowing; it requires a non-rational way of knowing. Table 3 (on the next page) summarizes the movement of the new spirituality.

So transcendence ceases to have a vertical dimension, in reference to God, and assumes a primarily horizontal relationship. It refers to a non-rational experience that creates a nonhierarchical sense of connection between people and the rest of creation. To put it in another way, the divine is no longer apart from the world but immanent within it. And the way of knowing this spiritual transcendence is not reason but experience and feeling.

**Table 3.** Movements in Today's Spirituality

| From<br>The Old Dualism | Toward<br>The New Holism |
|---|---|
| up-down (hierarchy) | horizontal relationship |
| inner-outer | holistic |
| self-nature | interconnectedness |
| self-others | intimacy |
| disparate | unified |
| rational detachment | sensuous attachment |
| external spirituality | immanent spirituality |

## The Migration to Experience

The spirituality we are describing aims to overcome the destructive dualisms of modernity and reconnect people with a deep spiritual reality within the world. But it does so at an immense intellectual price. By abandoning reason in favor of feeling and experience, it discards one set of dualisms for another.

C. S. Lewis's book *The Pilgrim's Regress* is helpful here.[2] Playing on John Bunyan's famous allegory, Lewis examines the intellectual history of Europe. In the story a straight road runs through the center of a country. This is orthodox Christianity. But it is possible to explore the territory to the north and south of this road. The north represents realism, rationalism, systematization and the exclusive use of reason, while moving south one would move further and further into feeling, experience, mysticism and naturalism. Lewis described it this way:

The Northerners are men of rigid systems whether sceptical or dogmatic, Aristocrats, Stoics, Pharisees, Rigorists, signed and sealed members of highly organized 'Parties'. The Southerners are by their very nature less definable; boneless souls whose doors stand open day and night to almost every visitant, . . . the smudging of all frontiers, the relaxation of resistances, dreams, opium, darkness, death, and the return to the womb. Every feeling is justified by the mere fact that it is felt: for a

Northerner, every feeling on the same ground is suspect. An arrogant and hasty selectiveness on some narrow a priori basis cuts him off from the sources of life.... I take our own age to be predominantly Northern.[3] Much has changed since Lewis's time, but his basic schema is helpful to our discussion. What has changed is that, first, the main road has been almost removed. Traditional Christianity is no longer that highway cutting through the center of Western culture. Modernity has no guiding road but two territories: Lewis's North and South. Second, with the breakdown of modernity there is a massive shift in dominance from the North to the South, from post-Enlightenment rationalism and realism to the realm of intuition, feeling, experience and an immanent mysticism.

Today's search for transcendence is a massive shift to the South: from rationalism to intuitionism, from objectivity to mystification, from fact to myth, from disparate realities to a new monism, from the domination of humankind to a new domination of a reenchanted nature, from detachment to sensuous attachment, from objective analysis to mythological description. Mystical communion and connectedness have become the roads along which this spiritual quest moves.

Some brief comments on the presence of Eastern mysticism will illustrate the point we are making. The appeal of this spirituality is that it offers people a means of transcending their rational, analytic faculties. These are no longer deemed the primary modes of knowing one's place in the universe. Eastern spiritualities emphasize developing a state of detachment through a series of techniques for emptying oneself of all material desires and needs. While this sounds like the opposite of the desire for unitiveness we have been describing, it isn't. The purpose of such detachment is connection with a higher, cosmic consciousness, described as enlightenment, the experience of oneness with all things.

The question we must ask is not so much what Eastern mysticism teaches, but why do people in Western culture find themselves attracted to its technologies of higher consciousness? It is not, primarily, a reaction to technology (although that is present). Eastern mystical practices are full of their own techniques; that is part of their attraction. And it is not simply that people are looking for some spiritual means of survival in a highly secular environment, although this too is involved.

People are attracted to Eastern mysticism principally because they long to transcend the separateness believed to be rooted in our thought-forms and practiced in our traditional spiritualities. They are grafting into their belief systems spiritualities that seem to connect them with the cosmic whole. This is what we mean by the search for transcendence.

Gregory Bateson illustrated this approach in his book *Angels Fear: Toward an Epistemology of the Sacred*.[4] The more Bateson explored the unity of nature,[5] the more he became aware of what he called the presence of the sacred. He searched for a monism that would replace the Cartesian separation of mind and matter. This monism was to be the key to an integration of Western science and a new spiritual awareness of the sacredness that lies behind all things.

Here the term *sacred*, like *transcendence*, is used to express an inner, connected unity in all of life which is more experienced than rationally observed. This experience is the belief that our minds and nature form a single unity, in which there is no mind separate from body and no god separate from creation. What is being advocated is a renewed sensuous relationship with nature. The experience of the sensuous is then interpreted as a spiritual, transcendent reconnection with our external environment.

All of this is suggestive of the Romantic period of the last century. One is reminded of Wordsworth's *Prelude* without its more dark and threatening elements. Today such reconnection is all light and hope. In the words of Andrew Greeley, it is being fueled by "a deep disenchantment, or boredom, with science and rationalism—a feeling reflected in our society's growing interest in mysticism, spirituality and belief in the paranormal."[6]

Often this quest results in a confused Lego-Land spirituality where beliefs are shaped from a variety of systems and grafted onto a form of Christianity. In a recent workshop for Canadian Baptists, a largely evangelical body, one man responded to comments about Christians' failure to address the problems of the earth by suggesting that Matthew Fox's book *The Coming of the Cosmic Christ* provided an answer. Far from an orthodox, evangelical understanding of biblical faith, the book's perspective is a mixture of neopaganism with Christianity.

In the same workshop a very honest woman expressed her confusion. She was unsure how to make sense of all she was learning and how she could integrate it into Christianity. She told the group that she had just spent a week with an ecofeminist; she had learned about goddess worship and mystical union with nature.

These workshop participants are genuinely concerned Christians trying to make sense of their faith. They too are searching for a connective, unifying spirituality. They do this by grafting other perspectives onto their Christianity.

### The Church's Response

How will the gospel be heard in this confusing search for direction? We hear a lot about how to reach baby boomers and baby busters, about the megachurches and supermarket Christianity. We have studied the TV generation to death and offered churches myriad new techniques to produce growth. But it is becoming clear that much of our vaunted growth and success in evangelical churches is growth by transfer, the famous circulation of the saints. We are still missing the bulk of the population who sense that something is profoundly wrong with our culture and search for a spirituality to make sense of it all. They no longer want programs catering to their every need, but a spirituality that will address the serious issues facing the world.

In the imagery of C. S. Lewis's allegory, our culture is rapidly migrating to the South. But the church must not simply "read the culture," sense where it is moving and join the rush into experience and romantic connectedness. Lewis was correct in calling for Christians to keep on the road that straddles North and South.

We have long lived in the North; our gospel has been shaped by post-Enlightenment rationalism. But the road south will no more lead our culture into a future of hope than did all the materialist promises of a secular utopia in the journey north. Exchanging one for the other will only lead to the same results by a different path: alienation, confusion and a broken world. Only the biblical revelation of God's transcendent power to heal creation in Jesus Christ by making all things new can offer any kind of enduring hope in these difficult times. But this will require Christians to rethink and reexperience the Gospel. What we require is a Christianity that is *both* deeply rational and profoundly experiential—totally committed to God's transcendence and deeply incarnational so that people can be reconnected to place, and to earth itself, in a healed creation.

The focus of this final section is upon liturgy, the way we worship. At a fundamental level worship carries the idea of binding back together what has been fragmented. It is the means, process and context in which all of life is bound back together. Worship is not just a personal relationship between God and the individual, but a living encounter through which all creation is bound back to its Creator. In this sense, worship is an eminently suitable process by which to engage the emerging spirituality.

Worship creates a reality that cannot exist without its presence. It is essential to a unitive, whole experience of life; it is the key to corporate connectedness and belonging. For these reasons, the most profound apologetic the church can make to this search for transcendence is the recovery of the rich depth of Christian worship.

What follows is not an exposition of new ways of worship, nor is it an attempt to unfold a comprehensive account of worship; rather, it is a series of direction-pointers, hints along the way, for engagement with today's secular spirituality.

Two movements within the church contribute to my discussion. One evidences some manifestations of the culture's move toward Lewis's South; the other represents a healthy expression of Northern living. I will suggest our worship needs to include both these directions. The first movement we will look at is the Vineyard, led by John Wimber. The second is Eastern Orthodox liturgical theology.

## The Vineyard Movement
The Vineyard is illustrative of numerous renewal movements in the modern world—the charismatic and neo-Pentecostal renewal in North America as well as the burgeoning house-church movement in the United Kingdom. The emphasis is upon direct experience of God through the Spirit. The Vineyard's worship theology lays great stress on immediacy and intimacy of the believer with Jesus.

John Wimber and the Vineyard shape their worship around the belief that we must experience reality in a new way. Marilyn Ferguson's call to get outside our old, limited way of perceiving finds a counterpart in the Vineyard. Wimber calls Western Christians to a paradigm shift in their understanding of the world. This involves looking beyond modernity. Building on the work of missionary anthropologist Charles Kraft, Wimber argues that the worldview of modernity is closed, materialist and rationalist in structure, excluding the supernatural from the natural world. He suggests that a more biblical worldview—a worldview that can be found in the church outside Europe and North America—sees the natural and the supernatural as interpenetrated. Wimber's paradigm shift would enable Western Christians to have a whole new experience of God. He is not inviting Christians into an *irrational* experience, but he argues that biblically there are ways of knowing beyond Western rationalism.

The Vineyard movement, with its emphasis upon signs and wonders, puts this paradigm shift into practice. Attempts are made to recover and redefine such spiritual gifts as words of knowledge, prophecy, healing, dreams and visions. Every Christian is called to be involved in prayer for healing and open to receive "pictures" or "words" that represent God's direction. When Christians grasp this new, biblical paradigm, Wimber teaches, they will be a powerful force for evangelism.

There are many questions about the practice of signs and wonders, and caution is important. People have received "words" and used them to heal someone at the point of death within non-Christian groups. One must also question the cognitive dissonance between the Vineyard's claims and the reality. Well-intentioned people have used these teachings to do bizarre and damaging things to people.

But there is an important element of truth in the claim that the church must reflect on its captivity to the worldview of modernity and risk exploring other ways of knowing the working of God in our world.

The spiritual search we have described is shaping beliefs—not that people are joining organizations, but that they are open to alternative ways of seeing this world. We need to rediscover the transcendent God who is wholly other but also *present,* found not only in the unassailable recesses of our hearts but also in the materiality of life. This is not a call to monism, seeing God as a part of nature. But we must recover an experience of God's presence and involvement in the world. The incarnational character of the gospel must be taken seriously if we are to practice a responsive spirituality. At this point the Vineyard contributes to a worship life that directs people to an experience of the transcendent God who is with us.

A second theme emerging from the Vineyard is *intimacy.* The term refers to an attitude and expectation in worship. It relates to the sense of liturgy as a binding together in an experience of God's presence. Intimacy is not an issue of style as much as a matter of understanding the nature of worship. It is the desire and intention to meet with God in a deep, personal way as his children. In worship God is not just an idea whom we address with rational theological statements assuring him of his identity. Intimacy is connection at a profoundly experiential level with the Lord of the Universe and with one another.

People in the Vineyard speak of inviting the Spirit to be present, or of God's coming in a felt, experienced manner. Along with a growing number of others, Wimber would say that evangelical worship is often bereft of any experience of God. Our liturgies are correct and theologically appropriate, but somehow there is no encounter with the living God, no binding and unitive experience of the community with the transcendent Presence who is God. Intimacy with God comes out of the longing to be connected with the wholeness of life. As such, it is an important and long-neglected element of worship in our cultural context. If there were a greater experience of God's presence, an expectation of intimacy, of knowing ourselves corporately connected to God and hearing ourselves addressed by God in ways not limited to a sermon, then our worship could be a means of mission to a spiritually hungry and disconnected culture.

There is a problem of balance, of course. I am not advocating worship based simply on experience and feelings of God's presence. This would be unhealthy, saccharine and empty of content. It would create a minimalist spirituality shaped by the latest sense of God's speaking through someone or a dependence upon some new prophetic movement. The emphasis upon intimacy, unless carefully balanced by a strong sense of mission and reaching beyond the self, leads to an unsettling Christian narcissism that feeds the need for experience and escape. This is already taking place in churches with poor, unreflective leadership.

But surely there is, in the midst of our well-controlled and highly rational worship, a place for direct experience of God. At this point the Vineyard has some things to teach us. An intense longing for something that can only be called the transcendent is emerging in our culture. We must reconnect people with an experience of the transcendent God who has come to us in Jesus Christ.

I remember when that first occurred for me in worship. I had been a pastor for eight years, leading a congregation in worship every Sunday but rarely feeling that the experience went beyond human words and nineteenth-century hymns on the organ. Then, in 1979, I spent a week with David Watson in York, England. Watson was a bright, thoughtful man of God. As I talked with him, even the skeptic in me knew that I was not dealing with an intellectual lightweight. I had to listen to this Anglican and take seriously what he was saying about the work of God in his congregation.

I will never forget the first evening I worshiped in his congregation. The building was crammed full of people of all ages, but mostly in their thirties and forties. I entered the service as an observer because, even though the Book of Common Prayer was familiar to me from my childhood, it was all so different. Something profoundly deep and moving was occurring. I was watching *worship*, and I knew that I had never experienced this before, even though I had been involved in worship for many years as a leader. I knew God's presence in a powerful and intimate way that evening and discovered that this need not be some unusual experience that occurs only rarely in one's life. My journey into worship had begun.

In an age when people are hungering to be reconnected with life, Christians have the very Bread of Life to share, not just in words but in the experience of encounter and intimacy with God. We have not begun to recover the missiological depth of worship for our engagement with this culture. The charismatic renewal has much to teach us, and I thank God for the fresh winds of the Spirit that are moving through the church.

Recovering an expectation of intimacy and spiritual giftings could help congregations encounter people as they move from rationalism toward feeling and experience, from the North to the South. We need to demonstrate how people can experience a healing transcendence in God. But we must carefully keep to the balanced center. The historic Christian traditions can help us here. For worship must not only reconnect us to the experience of God, it must also reconnect us with the earth.

### Eastern Orthodox Theology of Worship

Worship can be shaped by fads. Some renewal movements make intimacy an end in itself. Worship is more than singing intimate songs to the Lord for fifteen minutes, listening to a sermon and then calling the Spirit to be present. Indeed, I am concerned by the degree to which this style of worship can become separated from traditions formed out of serious attempts to make God's presence *in the world* genuinely known and experienced.

Insights from Orthodox worship could help in the recovery of a worship life that roots spirituality in the creation. This is not to suggest the adoption of Orthodox *practices*, for practice is not so much the issue as is the theology behind it. An Orthodox understanding of worship can help us bind people back to God, one another and the natural world.

In the search for a spiritual direction, transcendence is often replaced by immanence. In part this is because of the dichotomy that emerged in Western Christendom between the sacred and the profane, the spiritual and the material. The arena of God's influence was narrowed, and the gospel reduced to concern for immaterial souls. The natural world, emptied of mystery, became only matter subject to exploitation and devoid of spiritual reality. The symbol of food in the Big Carrot is fitting because the new spiritualities reconnect people with the earth, and food is about our earth-connectedness; it is a sacrament of the earth, a symbol of earth care.

The discussion that follows uses Alexander Schmemann's brilliant work *For the Life of the World* as a primary resource.[7] Schmemann begins his book, which is about worship in the Orthodox tradition, with a discussion of food and its place in the Bible. He suggests that the phrase "a man is what he eats" is, in fact, the definition of humankind given by the Bible. In the creation story Adam is first presented as a hungry being, and the whole of the Garden, except one tree, is presented as his food. In order to live, we must take the world into our body and transform it into our own flesh and blood. Therefore, we are what we eat, the whole world is given as a banquet table, and the image of banquet is a central scriptural metaphor for God's re-creating activity.

Schmemann wants to answer a basic question: "Of what life do we speak, what life do we preach, proclaim and announce when, as Christians, we confess that Christ died for the life of the world?"[8] He identifies two possible responses. On one side are those who say that the life we are talking about is the religious life, a world to itself apart from the "secular world." This life is found in the inner recesses of the soul; it is the subjective personal salvation of contemporary evangelicalism. This form of religious life sees the secular, the life of eating and drinking, as irrelevant and deprives it of any real meaning. This answer to the question: "What life do we proclaim?" results in worship disconnected from the material world.

But there are those who answer the question with the opposite response: to make the world better. This is the call to leave the worship center and enter the world with a secular religion.

Schmemann insists that neither group adequately answers the question of what we mean when we say that Jesus came for the life of the world. Each operates within a basic dichotomy between the sacred and the profane, the spiritual and the material. Each merely chooses its side. But these dichotomies do not exist in the Scriptures. In the Bible the world that is given by God as food to be made into flesh and blood is also the world through which human beings know communion with God. They are one and the same world. The world is divine love made food. So human beings are called to bless God for all of life and to be priests in the midst of creation. The whole world was created as one great sacrament, one blessing and sign of God, and humanity is the priesthood of this cosmic sacrament.

This understanding of spirituality has been neglected in evangelical life and worship. We have ceased to recognize how we have been created hungry for God alone, and how the world is a sacrament of communion with God. This recognition turns us from dematerialized spirituality toward the realization that we encounter God in and through the material. Worship leads us into a life filled with God in the midst of the materiality of life.

The world was never intended to be just "material," matter devoid of life. It is the sacrament of God's presence; it is food. Everything that exists makes God known to us and enables communion with God. Because God blesses everything he creates, all creation is a sign of his presence and love. Here is a spirituality that brings mystery, connectedness and unity back into the relationship between humankind and nature. The world is the incarnational locus of God's meeting with us.

In this Orthodox perspective, worship is not limited to our relationship with God above and outside of nature. It is a worship intimately connected to the world. The world is the sacramental place where we experience God, a part of the creation that is being redeemed into the wholeness of Christ. Without the material world there can be no communion with God. But conversely, without communion with God there can be no understanding of what the world is about in all its interconnectedness.

Orthodox theology unfolds a worship that connects humanity, God and the world. If the world is a sacrament and banquet of God's presence, then worship can communicate something profoundly important to our culture. *Banquet* is a word that conveys joy. Our liturgies are to be full of the joy of the Lord's life in and for this world, rather than merely the expectation of a world to come. Perhaps we need to recover the Christian calendar, to celebrate the great feasts as times of joy and proclamation of our Lord in the world. Feast days could function as symbols of how all of life is organically related to the rhythms of nature.

Schmemann also speaks about the meaning of baptism in worship. If we limit baptism to a spiritual sign and forget how physical an event it is, we continue the dichotomy between the material and the spiritual. Baptism has to do with water and with God's Spirit entering the physical reality of a body, that life-breathing earth and mud called humanity, so that a transformation occurs. In baptism we symbolize the abolition of the opposition between the sacred and profane.

In this theology of worship human beings are called to be the priests of a creation that is no longer a thing to be used. Rather, it is the "sacrament of the Kingdom."[9] Transcendence, the longing for unitive connectedness, will not come through a reduction of God to some immanent process in the world, nor can creation be freed from its destructive bondage by being divinized. The longing for connectedness and the healing of a broken earth require that we bind ourselves back, in worship, to the living God. In this life, the life of Christ given for the life of the whole world, is the church's most powerful response to the search for transcendence.

# Evangelism in a Time of Change

I began my study of the Carrot Common with the assumption that I faced a rather simple task of designing evangelism strategies for a local neighborhood. What I discovered is that effective evangelism requires a careful reading of context, because the modern world is undergoing a process of profound change. This change involves both rejection and transformation. In the search for paradigms, a worldview is being shaped which moves modernity away from the Christianity of the post-Enlightenment period. So God's people must recover the gospel for a changing time.

Novelist Don DeLillo's bestseller *Mao II* characterizes our culture as crowded with lonely, isolated individuals and controlled by religious cults and terrorist groups. The book begins with a mass marriage of thousands of young couples by the Reverend Sun Myung Moon, leader of the Unification Church. The event actually occurred in Madison Square Garden in 1982. In DeLillo's account the stadium is filled with anxious, confused parents straining to identify a son or daughter in the swirling mass of anonymous couples. One father muses over the event and reflects: "When the Old God leaves the world, what happens to all the unexpended faith?"[1]

For many the "Old God" has left the world, but faith and the need to believe have not disappeared. The loss of our "Old God" is not simply a turning away from Christian theism. It is the loss of faith in a promised technological utopia and the hope that rational control would lead us to a better world. So unexpended faith is swirling about looking for somewhere to root itself, some new "god" to satisfy its hunger.

Today's church is in crisis. Its renewal requires far more than liturgical change or doctrinal correction. Focusing on new structures or fresh prophecies is an important but inadequate response. The tectonic plates of Western culture are shifting. As modernity is questioned and parts of it rejected, the church is also questioned and marginalized.

An anguished search is shaping our culture. People look for spiritual foundations on which to rebuild lives that have been fragmented. The church is not seen as a credible alternative. So the fundamental question for the church in North America is missiological: How will the gospel be heard? How may God's songs be sung in a strange land?

### Recovering a Passionate Vision

We must recover a passionate vision of God's purpose in the world. Our time yearns for people who see a future—not just survival, a pulling back from the brink of destruction, but a healed creation. It will be people with a passionate conviction of God's power to transform our present situation who will evangelize today.

We have witnessed the abandonment of the idea that some underlying belief system can bring hope. Instead, people have opted for personal fulfillment and the cult of relevance to escape from fragmentation. And most of our churches, of either the right or the left, have positioned themselves to respond to these escapist wishes. Whether with a gospel of personal fulfillment in Jesus or of accommodation to the latest movement for liberation, we have opted for the cultural norm. We have lost the vision of a cosmic, transforming Christ who addresses all of life because, at the resurrection, history was changed. Lost is the conviction that we are in the times of the end, when God is bringing to completion a new heaven and a new earth in which all brokenness, fragmentation and sin will be overcome.

Without a vision the people perish. To evangelize our culture for Jesus Christ we must step away from being the chaplains of people, from proffering an individualistic, needs-centered, user-friendly gospel, and recover the transforming vision that is resident in the heart of the gospel.

## A Commitment to Listen

Effective evangelism will require a commitment to listening. Throughout this book the principle of contextualization has been emphasized. Our problem is not the inadequacy of the gospel but the fact that we have forgotten how to read the gospel through the realities of the context. Adequate listening demands that we hear the deep concerns shaping our time.

This is more than reading Gallup polls or gathering psychographics. These are useful tools, but by themselves they will not create a reflective community of God's people. The danger of these approaches is that they may tempt us to create a gospel that merely matches itself up to the current trends, a gospel captive to culture with no transforming power. In the short run, such approaches can be highly successful. They can fill church buildings. But the listening we need requires more than a reading of statistics, trends and felt needs.

We require the hard listening of the mind which plumbs the heart of this culture. Such listening will enable us to rediscover the gospel as God's good news for our context. As Schreiter's model of contextualization stresses, such listening does not diminish the gospel but allows it to speak with power and clarity. The combination of a passionate, biblically centered vision of God's purposes with an intelligent and credible process of listening will create an evangelism with integrity and meaning for our time.

### Refocusing the Church's Life

Despite all our protestations, the church in North America remains focused upon itself. Until this is changed, evangelization will continue to look like forays into the world in order to recruit members for our clubs. We must refocus the life of the church from the inside to the outside.

Lesslie Newbigin has said this best in the concluding chapters of his book *The Gospel in a Pluralist Society*. The congregation of Christ's people does not exist to shiver in the cold of humiliation, hiding away from the offense of the world. But neither does it exist to create a treadmill of programs to keep the faithful busy in the belief that they are accomplishing God's purposes by keeping the lights on at the church building seven days a week. We need to start switching the lights off, locking the doors and disbanding the programs. This is not where God's people are called to be, and it is not the journey Jesus Christ has invited them to undertake.

Newbigin asks what kind of ministerial leadership will nourish the people of God for engagement with a changing society. Ministerial leadership is not primarily called to look after the people of a congregation. Not at all. If a congregation exists for its neighborhood and not for itself, then the calling of leadership is to move out ahead, to refocus the congregation's life from itself to the context in which it is found. We need missionary leaders in our churches, not chaplains. We need pastors who lead their people from the front, who, like Jesus, can say with integrity, "Follow me."[2] Refocusing the church away from itself and into its context is a need critical for evangelism today.

### Congregations as Pilgrim Communities

It is not a contradiction to say that the church must refocus its life outside itself and, at the same time, recover the sense of being a pilgrim community. Indeed, the former demands the latter, and the latter only has vital life in the former. Community demands a pilgrim band who are on a journey, caught up in something fantastically bigger than themselves and their needs.

I have encountered the pain within myself—pain that reaches far back into childhood, pain that has emerged through all kinds of relationships. Some of that pain will never be removed except by Christ himself when I stand, finally, in his presence, the glass wiped clean, the glory no longer reflected. His shining beauty will make me whole. Our attempts to create community around a gospel of self-fulfillment and meeting personal needs is narcissistic and will offer no real healing. Healing and wholeness are located in knowing that I am on the way, that I have been caught up in something much greater than my struggles.

In the immensity of God's purposes for all of creation my struggle takes on its proper perspective. We need communities of God's people bound to one another because they have discovered the One in their midst who takes up their pain and gives it meaning in the larger call of a great journey toward a transformed and healed creation.

## A Worshiping Community

Finally, and best of all, it is a worshiping community that will evangelize our culture. There is no more profound apologetic for the gospel than the vitality of a people at worship. All that we have said to this point is but a footnote to this essential element. Our culture needs to see communities of God's people so convinced of God's future in Christ that they worship with boldness, announcing the "already" of that future as it impinges upon the present.

But we must discover a worship that speaks to the people outside the walls of our buildings. We must risk letting go of styles and forms that keep our worship from being a missionary announcement. In the end, worship is not for us; it is the people of God addressing their Lord in such a way that neighborhoods know that the God of creation who has met us in Jesus

Christ is present and cannot be dismissed into irrelevance.

These are difficult days for the church. We are invited on a journey, to take our harps from the trees and sing the Lord's song in a strange land. The road ahead will change us profoundly. But only by traveling that road will we discover that the Lord redeems his people and his world in the midst of changing times.

# Notes

### Introduction: The Big Carrot

[1]Peter Drucker, *The New Realities: In Government and Politics, in Economics and Business, in Society and World View* (New York: Harper & Row, 1989), pp. 3-4.

[2]O. B. Hardison Jr., *Disappearing Through a Skylight: Culture and Technology in the Twentieth Century* (New York: Penguin Books, 1989), p. 5.

[3]Anita Gordon and David Suzuki, *It's a Matter of Survival* (Toronto: Stoddart, 1990), p. 1.

[4]Ibid., p. 53.

[5]Robert Ornstein and Paul Ehrlich, *New World, New Mind* (New York: Simon & Schuster, 1989), p. 12.

[6]Diogenes Allen, *Christian Belief in a Postmodern World: The Full Wealth of Conviction* (Louisville, Ky.: Westminster/John Knox Press, 1989).

[7]James B. Miller, "The Emerging Postmodern World," *Postmodern Theology: Christian Faith in a Pluralist World*, ed. Frederic B. Burnham (San Francisco: Harper & Row, 1989), p. 1.

[8]Robert Wuthnow, *The Restructuring of American Religion: Society and Faith Since World War*

*II* (Princeton, N.J.: Princeton University Press, 1988), chap. 11.

⁹Statistics still map a decline in church attendance. David Barrett estimates that in North America and Europe 53,000 people leave the church each week never to return. See David Barrett, *World Christian Encyclopedia* (London: Oxford University Press, 1982), p. 7. Peter Brierly (*Christian England* [London: MARC Europe, 1991]) estimates that in the United Kingdom between 1979 and 1989 over a thousand members were leaving the church in England every week. As Reginald Bibby shows (*Fragmented Gods: The Poverty and Potential of Religion in Canada* [Toronto: Irwin, 1987]), total denominational membership in Canada between 1926 and 1985 went from 16.4 percent of the total population to 9.5 percent.

¹⁰Peter Schineller, *A Handbook on Inculturation* (New York: Paulist Press, 1990), p. 22.

¹¹Thomas Oden, "Back to the Fathers," interview by Christopher Hall, *Christianity Today,* September 24, 1990, pp. 28-31.

### Chapter 1: Change, Growth, Challenge

¹John Naisbitt and Patricia Aburdene, *Megatrends 2000: Ten New Directions for the 1990's* (New York: Avon Books, 1990), p. 296.

²Kathryn Knight, "Activism Through Entrepreneurship," *Common Ground,* Winter 1987, p. 6.

³Ibid., p. 5.

⁴Shiatsu is an Eastern technique for healing which has become increasingly popular among those seeking a holistic, nonintrusive, "natural" form of healing. On the premise that the body is made up of interconnected energy fields, Shiatsu therapy is applied to specific areas of the feet to stimulate healing mechanisms in other parts of the body.

### Chapter 2: Making the World a Better Place

¹James W. Sire, *The Universe Next Door: A Basic World View Catalog* (Downers Grove, Ill.: InterVarsity Press, 1976), p. 17.

### Chapter 3: A Worldview Is Rejected

¹Colin E. Gunton, *Enlightenment and Alienation: An Essay Towards a Trinitarian Theology* (Grand Rapids, Mich.: Eerdmans, 1985).

²Lesslie Newbigin, *Foolishness to the Greeks: The Gospel and Western Culture* (Grand Rapids, Mich.: Eerdmans, 1985); *The Gospel in a Pluralist Society* (Grand Rapids, Mich.: Eerdmans, 1989).

³George Parkin Grant, *Technology and Justice* (Toronto: Anansi Press, 1986), pp. 15-16.

⁴Hardison, *Disappearing Through a Skylight,* p. 178.

⁵Thomas Berry, *The Dream of the Earth* (San Francisco: Sierra Club Books, 1990), p. 17.

⁶Frances Fitzgerald, *Cities on a Hill: A Journey Through Contemporary American Cultures* (New York: Simon & Schuster, 1987), p. 387.

⁷Naisbitt and Aburdene, *Megatrends 2000,* pp. 296-97.

⁸See Brierly, *Christian England.*

[9]Anna Marie Aagaard, "Mission Tomorrow: Nothing Will Be Easy," in *Mission in the 1990's*, ed. Gerald H. Anderson, James M. Phillips and Robert T. Coote (Grand Rapids, Mich.: Eerdmans, 1991), p. 20.

## Chapter 4: The Church and Shifting Worldviews

[1]Fritjof Capra, *The Turning Point: Science and Society and the Rising Culture* (New York: Simon & Schuster, 1982), pp. 411-12.

[2]Matthew Fox, *The Coming of the Cosmic Christ: The Healing of Mother Earth and the Birth of a Global Renaissance* (San Francisco: Harper & Row, 1988), p. 6.

[3]Carolyn Merchant, *The Death of Nature* (New York: Harper & Row, 1989).

[4]Gordon and Suzuki, *It's a Matter of Survival*, p. 53.

[5]Jürgen Moltmann, *God in Creation: An Ecological Doctrine of Creation* (London: S.C.M. Press, 1985).

[6]Prior to the development of the scientific revolution and its flowering in the post-Enlightenment period, Christian theology had been dominated by an Augustinian view of creation with a strong neo-Platonic content. Thus the natural world represented a sacramental microcosm. Creation symbolized and reflected the heavenly, eternal, spiritual reality. Nature was conceived of as the sacramental mirror through which one could look to see both God and spiritual reality. Nature had no function or meaning in and of itself. This medieval cosmology broke down at the beginning of the modern era.

The Reformation began to turn away from this sacramental cosmology as its doctrines gave a new meaning and place to the world. The notion of a world totally distinct from God enabled people to look at it with a whole new perspective. It gradually came to be seen as a thing in and for itself, thus opening the way for the development of the modern scientific method.

[7]Douglas John Hall, "The Significance of Grant's Cultural Analysis for Christian Theology in North America," in *George Grant in Process: Essays and Conversations*, ed. Larry Schmidt (Toronto: Anansi Press, 1978), p. 123.

[8]Ibid., pp. 123-24.

[9]Reginald Bibby, "Beyond Fragmentation," paper presented at McMaster Divinity College, Hamilton, Ontario, Canada, September 1988.

[10]More and more congregations are dwindling and aging, and their language and structures have little meaning to the larger culture. However, even if these sociocultural issues were addressed, of itself this would not change the point made in this section. The issues go deeper than speaking a community's language or reflecting its demographics. Seeker-sensitive services merely address the thin top layer, not the underlying forces of cultural change.

[11]Ronald M. Enroth, *The Lure of the Cults and the New Religions: Why They Attract and What We Can Do* (Downers Grove, Ill.: InterVarsity Press, 1987), pp. 41-42.

[12]Rodney Stark and William Sims Bainbridge, *The Future of Religion: Secularization, Revival and Cult Formation* (Los Angeles: University of California Press, 1987).

[13]Harvey Cox, *Turning East: The Promise and Peril of the New Orientalism* (New York: Simon

& Schuster, 1977), p. 100.

[14]James Turner, *Without God, Without Creed: The Origins of Unbelief in America* (Baltimore: Johns Hopkins University Press, 1985).

[15]Ibid., p. 140.

[16]Reginald Bibby, "Religionless Christianity: A Profile of Religion in the Canadian '80s," *Social Indicators Research* 13 (1983):1-16.

## Chapter 5: How Will the Gospel Be Heard?

[1]Stanley Hauerwas and William Willimon, *Resident Aliens: Life in the Christian Colony* (Nashville: Abingdon, 1989), pp. 15-17.

[2]John W. de Gruchy, *Theology and Ministry in Context and Crisis: A South African Perspective* (London: Collins, 1986), p. 158.

[3]Douglas John Hall, *Thinking the Faith: Christian Theology in a North American Context* (Minneapolis: Augsburg, 1989), p. 44.

[4]Robert J. Schreiter, *Constructing Local Theologies* (Maryknoll, N.Y.: Orbis Books, 1986).

## Chapter 6: Ecology

[1]Ilya Prigogine, *Order Out of Chaos: Man's New Dialogue with Nature* (Toronto: Bantam Books, 1984), p. 46.

[2]Ornstein and Ehrlich, *New World, New Mind.*

[3]This is, in part, what Matthew Fox argues for in his book *The Coming of the Cosmic Christ.*

[4]James Lovelock, *The Ages of Gaia: A Biography of Our Living Earth* (New York: W. W. Norton, 1988); Elisabeth Sahtouris, *Gaia: The Human Journey from Chaos to Cosmos* (Toronto: Simon & Schuster, 1989).

[5]Hall, *Thinking the Faith,* pp. 219-21.

[6]John E. Biersdorf, *Healing of Purpose: God's Call to Discipleship* (Nashville: Abingdon, 1985), p. 87.

[7]Thomas F. Torrance, *The Ground and Grammar of Theology* (Ottawa: Christian Journals Limited, 1980), p. ix.

[8]Newbigin, *Foolishness to the Greeks.*

[9]Albert Wolters, *Creation Regained: Biblical Basics for a Reformational Worldview* (Grand Rapids, Mich.: Eerdmans, 1985), p. 19.

[10]For the outline of this section I am indebted to the analysis of Paulos Mar Gregorios in his book *Cosmic Man: The Divine Presence* (New York: Paragon, 1988), a study of the fourth-century church father Gregory of Nyssa. See esp. pp. 223-26.

[11]Ibid., p. 224.

[12]Ibid., p. 225.

## Chapter 7: Community

[1]Laurence Shames, *The Hunger for More: Searching for Values in an Age of Greed* (New York: Random House/Vintage Books, 1991).

[2]Barbara Ehrenreich, *The Worst Years of Our Lives* (New York: Harper Perennial, 1990).

[3]*Harper's* 282 (February 1991).

[4]Ibid., p. 44.

[5]Anne Wilson Schaef and Diane Fassel, *The Addictive Organization* (New York: Harper & Row, 1988).

[6]Robert Bly, *Iron John: A Book About Men* (New York: Random House, 1990); Sam Keen, *Fire in the Belly* (New York: Bantam Books, 1991).

[7]Michael Ignatieff, *The Needs of Strangers* (London: Chatto & Windus/Hogarth Books, 1984), p. 139.

[8]Interview in *Omni* 13 (August 1991):86.

[9]Hauerwas and Willimon, *Resident Aliens,* pp. 49-55.

[10]Ibid., p. 52.

### Chapter 8: The New Spirituality

[1]*Omni* 13 (August 1991).

[2]C. S. Lewis, *The Pilgrim's Regress* (Glasgow, U.K.: Collins/Fount, 1990).

[3]Ibid., pp. 18-19.

[4]Gregory Bateson, *Angels Fear: Toward an Epistemology of the Sacred* (Toronto: Bantam Books, 1988).

[5]See his earlier work *Mind and Nature: A Necessary Unity* (Toronto: Bantam Books, 1980).

[6]*Psychology Today,* November 1989, p. 33.

[7]Alexander Schmemann, *For the Life of the World: Sacraments and Orthodoxy* (New York: St. Vladimir's Seminary Press, 1988).

[8]Ibid., pp. 11-12.

[9]Ibid., p. 93.

### Epilogue

[1]Don DeLillo, *Mao II* (New York: Viking, 1991), p. 7.

[2]Newbigin, *The Gospel in a Pluralist Society,* pp. 234-38.

# For Further Reading

Allen, Diogenes. *Christian Belief in a Postmodern World: The Full Wealth of Conviction.* Louisville, Ky.: Westminster/John Knox Press, 1989.

Anderson, Gerald H., James M. Phillips and Robert T. Coote, eds. *Mission in the 1990s.* Grand Rapids, Mich.: Eerdmans, 1991.

Barrett, David B. *World Christian Encyclopedia.* London: Oxford University Press, 1982.

Barrett, William. *Death of the Soul: From Descartes to the Computer.* New York: Anchor Books, 1987.

Bateson, Gregory. *Angels Fear: Toward an Epistemology of the Sacred.* Toronto: Bantam Books, 1988.

————. *Mind and Nature: A Necessary Unity.* Toronto: Bantam Books, 1980.

Bellah, Robert N., et al. *Habits of the Heart: Individualism and Commitment in American Life.* New York: Harper & Row, 1985.

Berman, Morris. *The Reenchantment of the World.* Toronto: Bantam New Age Books, 1988.

Berry, Thomas. *The Dream of the Earth.* San Francisco: Sierra Club Books, 1990.

Bibby, Reginald W. *Fragmented Gods: The Poverty and Potential of Religion in Canada.* Toronto: Irwin Publishing, 1987.

Bibby, Reginald W., and Donald C. Posterski. *The Emerging Generation: An Inside Look at Canada's Teenagers.* Toronto: Irwin Publishing, 1985.

Biersdorf, John E. *Healing of Purpose: God's Call to Discipleship.* Nashville: Abingdon, 1985.

Bloesch, Donald. *Essentials of Evangelical Theology,* vol. 1. New York: Harper & Row, 1978.

_____ . *Crumbling Foundations.* Grand Rapids, Mich.: Zondervan, 1984.

Bloom, Allan. *The Closing of the American Mind.* New York: Simon & Schuster, 1987.

Bly, Robert. *Iron John: A Book About Men.* New York: Random House, 1990.

Bridge, Donald. *Signs and Wonders Today.* Leicester, U.K.: Inter-Varsity Press, 1985.

Brierly, Peter. *Christian England.* London: MARC Europe, 1991.

Brown, Colin. *That You May Believe: Miracles and Faith—Then and Now.* Grand Rapids, Mich.: Eerdmans, 1985.

Burnham, Frederic B., ed. *Postmodern Theology: Christian Faith in a Pluralist World.* San Francisco: Harper & Row, 1989.

Capra, Fritjof. *The Turning Point: Science and Society and the Rising Culture.* New York: Simon & Schuster, 1982.

Chadwick, Owen. *The Secularization of the European Mind in the Nineteenth Century.* London: Cambridge University Press, 1985.

Cox, Harvey. *Turning East: The Promise and Peril of the New Orientalism.* New York: Simon & Schuster, 1977.

Davies, Paul. *God and the New Physics.* Markam, Ont.: Penguin Books, 1983.

De Gruchy, John. *Theology and Ministry in Context and Crisis: A South African Perspective.* London: Collins, 1986.

DeLillo, Don. *Mao II.* New York: Viking, 1991.

Dodds, E. R. *Pagan and Christian in an Age of Anxiety: Some Aspects of Religious Experience from Marcus Aurelius to Constantine.* Cambridge, U.K.: Cambridge University Press/Norton, 1965.

Donovan, Vincent J. *The Church in the Midst of Creation.* Maryknoll, N.Y.: Orbis Books, 1989.

Drucker, Peter F. *The New Realities: In Government and Politics, in Economics and Business, in Society and World View.* New York: Harper & Row, 1989.

Ehrenreich, Barbara. *The Worst Years of Our Lives.* New York: Harper Perennial, 1990.

Ellul, Jacques. *The Presence of the Kingdom.* New York: Seabury, 1967.

Enroth, Ronald M. *The Lure of the Cults and the New Religions: Why They Attract and What We Can Do.* Downers Grove, Ill.: InterVarsity Press, 1987.

Ferguson, Marilyn. *The Aquarian Conspiracy: Personal and Social Transformation in the 1980s.* Los Angeles: J. P. Tarcher, 1980.

Fitzgerald, Frances. *Cities on a Hill: A Journey Through Contemporary American Cultures.* New York: Simon & Schuster, 1987.

Fox, Matthew. *The Coming of the Cosmic Christ: The Healing of Mother Earth and the Birth of a Global Renaissance.* San Francisco: Harper & Row, 1988.

Gordon, Anita, and David Suzuki. *It's a Matter of Survival.* Toronto: Stoddart, 1990.

Granberg-Michaelson, Wesley, ed. *Tending the Garden: Essays on the Gospel and the Earth.* Grand Rapids, Mich.: Eerdmans, 1987.

Grant, George Parkin. *Technology and Justice.* Toronto: Anansi Press, 1986.

Gregorios, Paulos Mar. *Cosmic Man: The Divine Presence—The Theology of St. Gregory of Nyssa.* New York: Paragon House, 1988.

Groothuis, Douglas. *Unmasking the New Age.* Downers Grove, Ill.: InterVarsity Press, 1986.

Gunton, Colin E. *Enlightenment and Alienation: An Essay Towards a Trinitarian Theology.* Grand Rapids, Mich.: Eerdmans, 1985.

Hall, Douglas John. *Imaging God: Dominion as Stewardship.* Grand Rapids, Mich.: Eerdmans, 1986.

————. *Thinking the Faith: Christian Theology in a North American Context.* Minneapolis: Augsburg, 1989.

Happold, F. C. *Religious Faith and Twentieth-Century Man.* 1966; rpt. New York: Crossroads Books, 1981.

Hardison, O. B., Jr. *Disappearing Through a Skylight: Culture and Technology in the Twentieth Century.* New York: Penguin Books, 1989.

Hauerwas, Stanley. *The Peaceable Kingdom: A Primer in Christian Ethics.* Notre Dame, Ind.: University of Notre Dame Press, 1983.

Hauerwas, Stanley, and William Willimon. *Resident Aliens: Life in the Christian Colony.* Nashville: Abingdon, 1989.

Hexham, Irving, and Karla Poewe. *Understanding Cults and New Religions.* Grand Rapids, Mich.: Eerdmans, 1986.

Ignatieff, Michael. *The Needs of Strangers.* London: Chatto & Windus/Hogarth Books, 1984.

Keen, Sam. *Fire in the Belly.* New York: Bantam Books, 1991.

Lewis, C. S. *The Pilgrim's Regress.* Glasgow, U.K.: Collins, 1990.

Lovelock, James. *The Ages of Gaia: A Biography of Our Living Earth.* New York: Norton, 1988.

MacIntyre, Alasdair. *After Virtue: A Study in Moral Theology.* Notre Dame, Ind.: University of Notre Dame Press, 1984.

McDonagh, Sean. *To Care for the Earth: A Call to a New Theology.* Santa Fe, N.M.: Bear, 1987.

Merchant, Carolyn. *The Death of Nature.* New York: Harper & Row, 1989.

Moltmann, Jürgen. *God in Creation: An Ecological Doctrine of Creation.* London: S.C.M. Press, 1985.

Naisbitt, John, and Patricia Aburdene. *Megatrends 2000: Ten New Directions for the 1990's.* New York: Avon Books, 1990.

Newbigin, Lesslie. *Foolishness to the Greeks: The Gospel and Western Culture.* Grand Rapids, Mich.: Eerdmans, 1986.

————. *The Gospel in a Pluralist Society.* Grand Rapids, Mich.: Eerdmans, 1989.

Ornstein, Robert, and Paul Ehrlich. *New World, New Mind.* New York: Simon & Schuster, 1989.

Owens, Virginia Stem. *And the Trees Clap Their Hands: Faith, Perception and the New Physics.* Grand Rapids, Mich.: Eerdmans, 1983.

Pelikan, Jaroslav. *The Spirit of Eastern Christendom (600-1700)*. Vol. 2 of *The Christian Tradition: A History of the Development of Doctrine*. Chicago: University of Chicago Press, 1977.

Prigogine, Ilya. *Order Out of Chaos: Man's New Dialogue with Nature*. Toronto: Bantam Books, 1984.

Sire, James W. *The Universe Next Door: A Basic World View Catalog*. 2nd ed. Downers Grove, Ill.: InterVarsity Press, 1988.

Schaef, Anne Wilson, and Diane Fassel. *The Addictive Organization*. New York: Harper & Row, 1988.

Shames, Laurence. *The Hunger for More: Searching for Values in an Age of Greed*. New York: Random House, 1991.

Schineller, Peter. *A Handbook on Inculturation*. New York: Paulist Press, 1990.

Schmemann, Alexander. *For the Life of the World: Sacraments and Orthodoxy*. New York: St. Vladimir's Seminary Press, 1988.

Schmidt, Larry, ed. *George Grant in Process*. Toronto: Anansi Press, 1987.

Schreiter, Robert J. *Constructing Local Theologies*. Maryknoll, N.Y.: Orbis Books, 1985.

Snyder, Howard A. *The Problem of Wineskins: Church Structure in a Technological Age*. Downers Grove, Ill.: InterVarsity Press, 1976.

———. *The Community of the King*. Downers Grove, Ill.: InterVarsity Press, 1977.

———. *Liberating the Church: The Ecology of Church and Kingdom*. Downers Grove, Ill.: InterVarsity Press, 1983.

Snyder, Howard A., and Daniel V. Runyan. *Foresight: Ten Major Trends That will Dramatically Affect the Future of Christians and the Church*. Nashville: Nelson, 1986.

Stark, Rodney, and William Sims Bainbridge. *The Future of Religion: Secularization, Revival and Cult Formation*. Los Angeles: University of California Press, 1987.

Torrance, Thomas F. *The Ground and Grammar of Theology*. Ottawa: Christian Journals, 1980.

Toulmin, Stephen E. *The Return to Cosmology: Postmodern Science and the Theology of Nature*. Los Angeles: University of California Press, 1985.

Turner, James. *Without God, Without Creed: The Origins of Unbelief in America*. Baltimore: John Hopkins University Press, 1985.

Walsh, Brian J., and J. Richard Middleton. *The Transforming Vision: Shaping a Christian World View*. Downers Grove, Ill.: InterVarsity Press, 1984.

Wilkinson, Loren, ed. *Earthkeeping: Christian Stewardship of Natural Resources*. Grand Rapids, Mich.: Eerdmans, 1980.

Wimber, John. *Power Evangelism: Signs and Wonders Today*. London: Hodder and Stoughton, 1985.

Wolters, Albert M. *Creation Regained: Biblical Basics for a Reformational Worldview*. Grand Rapids, Mich.: Eerdmans, 1985.

Wuthnow, Robert. *The Restructuring of American Religion: Society and Faith Since World War II*. Princeton, N.J.: Princeton University Press, 1988.